MW00618517

# Successful Community Leadership

# and Organization

## A SKILLS GUIDE FOR VOLUNTEERS AND PROFESSIONALS

## John E. Tropman

NASW PRESS
National Association of Social Workers
Washington, DC

Jeane W. Anastas, PhD, LMSW, President
Elizabeth J. Clark, PhD, ACSW, MPH, Executive Director

First edition: *Successful Community Leadership: A Skills Guide for Volunteers and Professionals*, NASW Press, 1995

Cheryl Y. Bradley, *Publisher*
Sarah Lowman, *Project Manager*
Cara Schumacher, *Proofreader*
Lori Holtzinger, *Indexer*

*Cover by* Naylor Design
*Interior design by* Electronic Quill Publishing Services
*Printed and bound by* Victor Graphics, Inc.

**Library of Congress Cataloging-in-Publication Data**

Tropman, John E.
  Successful community leadership and organization : a skills guide for volunteers and professionals / John E. Tropman. — 2nd ed.
      p. cm.
  Rev. ed. of: Successful community leadership : a skills guide for volunteers and professionals. c1997.
  Includes bibliographical references and index.
  ISBN 978-0-87101-439-9
  1. Community organization—United States. 2. Community leadership—United States. 3. Group decision-making—United States. I. Tropman, John E. Successful community leadership. II. Title.
  HN90.C6T75  2012
  303.3'4—dc23

                                                              2012018014

Printed in the United States of America

The historian Howard Zinn suggested that:

When you have models of how people can come together, even for a brief period, it suggests it could happen for a longer period. When you think of it, that's the way things operate in the scientific world, so why not socially? As soon as the Wright brothers could keep a plane aloft for 27 seconds, everyone knew from that point on that a plane might be kept aloft for hours. It's the same socially and culturally . . . We've had countless incidents in history where people have joined together in social movements and created a spirit of camaraderie or a spirit of sharing and togetherness which have absented them, even momentarily, from the world of greed and domination. If true community can stay aloft for 27 seconds, it is only a matter of time before such a community can last for hours. Only a matter of time before a beloved community, as Martin Luther King, Jr. spoke of, can come into being.

—NEPO, 2009, pp. 8–9

# Table of Contents

# Preface

American society has a unique history. In terms of immigration trends, Protestants settled first and Catholics second, the reverse of European settlement patterns. Thus, no large organization, like the Catholic Church, set the tone for American settlement. Second, no aristocracy provided guidance (however much it may have been "misguidance") for settlement patterns. So, perhaps by default, American society was, from the outset, a communitarian society. In New England, for example, small church groups decided what they wanted to do, organized, and did it. Not everyone participating in these groups agreed with the action, so they splintered and formed sects. And more sects.

As American population grew, it moved west. Lore has it that the self-sufficient individual—"mountain men," like Davy Crockett, James Bowie, and others—led settlement.

But the mountain-man hypothesis cannot stand before the wagon-train experience. That is, most settlers moved west, not as lone individuals but in organized, interdependent groups.

American historian Daniel Boorstin (1958) pointed out a fundamental difference between the structure of migration *to* and *within* America. The first was a passive, individual experience for participants. They came on a boat. Sailors did the work. The second, migration within the country, was a participatory, community effort. Boorstin suggested that the need for cooperation (community organization) gave internal migrants a sense of community's vital importance. No one makes it on theory alone, individualistic ethos to the contrary. To Boorstin's assertion I would only add that the wagon-train experience simply continued the communitarian emphasis developed during early periods of Protestant settlement (as opposed to settlement influenced by corporate Catholicism). Community organization!

By the 1840s, as de Tocqueville (1841) pointed out, "associations" were a core element of American values and action. But by 2000, Putnam (2000) observed that Americans were "bowling alone." In a short 160 years, American character had shifted from a community orientation to what Riesman, Glazer, and Denney (1950) called "the lonely crowd."

Just what is community? A *community* is a group that is unified around some common elements. These sometimes-overlapping elements can be geographic location, ethnic identification, or an affiliation or place of work (for example, the university community). Each community shares a sense of common fate, as well.

Community does not just happen; it has to be built and tended. Thus, organization and leadership within the community are essential. And community organization and leadership require skills. This book discusses many of these skills, focusing particularly on leading community meetings and building high-quality community decisions.

Community decision making involves an attempt by community members, often with the help of community organizers, to make decisions that will improve the community's condition. A hallmark of the community organization and decision-making process is that the community decides which direction it wants to go and the projects it wants to undertake. However, community citizens often lack the skills to deal with elements of decision making or do not know what to do when participating in community decision-making groups.

The process of working together in a community is complex (Rothman, Erlich, & Tropman, 1995; Tropman, 1995) and involves the sharing of information. Although information sharing can be done virtually, face-to-face exchange often offers the possibility of more thorough, accurate communication.

The normative bases for decision legitimization (extent and depth of preference, implementation responsibility, expertise, and preference of those with power), the simultaneous presence of norms, and differential weighting all mean that effective group decision management is vital for both community professionals and volunteers. This book is designed to help everyone interested in community decision making do a better job.

What does *better* mean in this context? It means that decisions are made in a timely fashion. A good decision made too late is the same as no decision at all; it is a nondecision—a sort of "passive aggression" at the community level. Groups that never do anything soon lose their membership.

In this context, better also means that—along the qualitative continuum of poor, good, and excellent decisions—the decisions range between good and excellent. High-quality decision making occurs when a community interest is identified, circulated, and incorporated into the decision. For this to happen, community decision makers need at their disposal good techniques, courage, and goodwill. The techniques in this book will help community decision making and other group processes at work, church, or school move to the high-quality end of the continuum.

Ideas in this book draw from the experience of community groups and leaders as near as Ann Arbor and Glen Arbor, Michigan, and as far as Boston, Buffalo, Chicago, Madison, and Pittsburgh. The manuscript benefits from their wisdom.

## USING THIS GUIDE

This second edition updates the first edition and adds considerably more detail, including introductory chapters on the idea of community itself. For students and community leaders or organizers, a read-through of this book is appropriate if you have the time. Several sections refer to the tasks a community worker or citizen leader might perform (for example, staff duties are discussed in one place; meeting organizing is found in another). However, one needs to know the appropriate roles of the community worker or citizen leader in different leadership positions. Many people have leadership interest and the ability to engage others but have no idea what leaders are supposed to do. Professional and student community leaders and organizers can help educate a community in this regard using the information from this book. Other suggestions follow on how to best use this book.

## Skim It

First, skim through the book, becoming familiar with the parts and chapters. Mark places of interest to yourself or others. Use different colors to mark different kinds of information for quick access.

## Study Relevant Sections

Study relevant sections in detail. Some information will be immediately applicable to your group process. A chairperson should read the section on chairpersons; a member should read the section on members.

## Adopt Group Guidelines

A step toward developing public procedures is to review this book at an early group meeting and adopt it as a guideline for the community process. That adoption means that the group supports the general ideas, orientations, and principles. (For example, the group would support the principles that govern productive community processes and a particular structure for handling meetings). Many groups adopt procedural guides such as *Robert's Rules of Order* (1970). Though thorough, *Robert's Rules of Order* is narrowly focused and concerned primarily with introducing motions at large meetings. The procedures suggested in this book, however, address the widest compass of community interest.

## IN SUM

This book helps people know what to do when they are involved in community leadership. It is a sort of cookbook, with recipes for making communities better. It is based on the premise that excellence is never an accident. Well-functioning communities function well because people work at making them do so. And as communities function better, tensions are reduced, connection is established, and caring is expressed. I wish you every success as you implement the techniques that aid you and your colleagues in building and tending a caring, connected community.

*John Tropman*

# Part One
## Essential Elements of Community Organization

Community has played a vital role in American history. In the absence of an aristocratic tradition, community was the place where citizens exchanged information and resources, developed and enforced norms, and created and sustained meaning. Often these were religious communities, but a matrix of communities—communities of interest and communities of commitment, among others—also influenced the course of American history.

## COMMUNITY ORGANIZATION IN SOCIAL WORK

In social work, helping communities to change, improve, and become more viable has a history as old as the discipline itself. Community—both its problems and its growth—has been a part of discipline-wide social work discussions since the American Social Science Association meetings in the 1870s through the more recent National Conference of Charities and Corrections, and the National Conference of Social Welfare (Garvin & Cox, 1995; Lane, 1939).

## CITIES EXPERIENCED "DISORGANIZATION"

Community leaders, academic professionals, and citizens at large felt strongly that the trend toward urbanization and industrialization, which characterized the United States after the Civil War, was profoundly dis-organizing to the old, somewhat idealized, rural community (Schwartz, 1965; Wilensky & Lebeaux, 1956). They tended to view the city as the antithesis of community. In the city, the ties that bound were either bro-ken or failed to take root. Social problems—juvenile delinquency, urban crime, dependence on the dole, and unemployment—were seen as fail-ures of community, a result of community disorganization. What bet-ter solution to problems of community disorganization than attempts to organize community to rebuild the connections that bound individuals interdependently to each other (Bernard, 1968).

## COMMUNITY ORGANIZATION AS A SUBDOMINANT EMPHASIS

For all its historic presence in society, and in social work particularly, com-munity emphasis and community organization are often subordinated to more individualistic views about the solutions to social problems. Ameri-cans seem to prefer the mountain-man lore of western settlement to the more community-focused, wagon-train explanations of the historical record. For this reason, perhaps, casework (and to some extent group work) specializations have been more popular in schools of social work than have community organization and, later, administration, planning, and policy specializations. The reasons underlying these preferences are manifold, complex, and not completely clear.

Suffice it to say that Americans' penchant for individualism in sports and business, as well as their interest in rewarding good deeds and pun-ishing wrongdoers, also appears in the helping professions. Just as in medicine, where individual physician-provided care is preferred over systemwide care, public-health prevention, in social work. Individual counseling and other micro-level interventions are more popular than macro-level solutions.

Americans' preference for freedom and lack of intervention also appears in its emphasis on remediation rather than prevention. Practi-cally speaking, Americans tend to avoid preventive intervention, waiting instead until some problem has presented itself (Burk, 1965). This view emphasizes, then, remediation over prevention. To a certain extent, how-ever, social work's macro-level specializations (community organizing, administration, policy) focus a bit more on the preventive, rather than remedial, work.

Though emphasis on individualism and remediation produce social work practice dominated by interests in casework and counseling, there is, nonetheless, a long history of community focus as well. It is to this area that we now turn our attention.

This section contains three chapters. Chapter 1 focuses on definitions of community and considers the implications of these differences. Naturally, there are many situations in which definitions intersect, and the resulting intersections produce the community matrix.

Chapter 2 considers community development, community action, and community planning as three different approaches to successful community organization and leadership. These approaches overlap in a phased sense, since development, which addresses problems of community cohesion, usually occurs first. The second phase, community capability, blends existing groups into an effective unit focused on specific advocacy issues using community action. The third phase, community competence, blends elements of community action into an ongoing effort and uses community planning as its main tool. Chapter 3 examines stages of the successful community leadership and organizing process. As in many aspects of life (working out, eating, sleeping), community organizing has beginning, middle, and ending phases. Somewhat different skill sets are useful at each phase.

# Chapter 1
## Understanding Community Matrix and Community Stages

We live in a pluralism of communities, a community matrix, as it were. Communities, as mentioned, are bonds created by commonalities. What are these commonalities? What things can a group of people hold in common? They can, of course, vary, but familial, interest, location, belief, identification, or activity bonds, among others, are common (Fellin, 2000; Johnson & Tropman, 1979). Communities can also be formed around a personal feature or experience. Let's consider some examples.

### COMMUNITY PLURALISMS

#### Communities of Common Relationship

In one sense, the family might be the primary community. There are families of origin, families of creation, and extended families. These familial connections may extend over wide space and other societal divisions and, with the current emphasis on genealogy, may in some sense reach back in time. As interest in family legacy grows, these communities might extend into the future as well.

#### Communities of Common Interest

People can share common interest; this interest can be in sports, helping others, great books, travel, or any other common interest around which individuals within each interest sector can form a kind of community, building bonds of appreciation and connection between them. Common knowledge about the activity creates familiarity among members. People may engage in common activities as a result of shared interest, attending sporting events or meetings together. The phrase *community of interest* refers to this kind of communal bond.

### Communities of Common Location

Alternatively, individuals may share a common location. Typically, this kind of community is referred to as a geographic community. It may begin with a block or neighborhood and extend to a several-block area of a large city (the south side of Chicago, the north end of Boston, a barrio, or a ghetto). Common residence often leads to, or is linked with, common interests and interactions, which reinforce the bonds of common location.

### Communities of Common Belief

Another kind of community grows out of a common belief or identification. Often religious communities are of this nature, and the phrase "community of believers" refers to this collection of communal identifications. Beliefs are often linked to common identifications, especially ethnic ones (the African American community, the Italian community, the Jewish community). When an individual recognizes herself or himself as of Italian or Jewish or black ancestry and holds ideas, beliefs, interests, and locations very different from those who do not share these, an ethnic (or racial, or gender) subcommunity exists. The concept of subculture or subcommunity refers to ideas or identifications that arise when beliefs are present and identifications and behavior patterns (foods, holidays, and the like) are a defining characteristic of the group. The Jewish community, the Irish Catholic community, and the scientific community, are all examples of communities of common belief.

### Communities of Common Features

Similarly, the presence of a common identifying feature or quality can create communal identification. Red-haired individuals have a common identifying feature that might cause them to get together with each other and, at least, promotes a certain common identification. Other individuals with racial and ethnic features may also find themselves commonly identified, even if they may not feel such a common identification.

Individuals who share an affliction or a disease may also form a community of common feature.

## Communities of Common Action or Activity

Communities may form around common activities. The organizational community or the community of the workplace is a prime example. Individuals who hold the same kind of job or work in the same place may form social roots or form unions to press for better working conditions and more pay. These individuals may have little else in common but the time that they spend together, day in and day out, over a series of years. The bond created by this kind of interaction can become a very strong community (King, 1997).

## COMMUNITY MATRIX

As must be evident by now, we are all members of many different types of communities. These individual elements or features are related to particular kinds of communities. The communities that are most powerful to us often develop when several types of community exist together. Hence, people with common beliefs often live near each other, creating a subcultural and geographic bond. Similarly, areas of a city are identified by race, class, or other common characteristics. Thus, specific community identifications tend to reinforce each other.

## COMMUNITY CONFLICT

Communities, because of the element of commitment that is involved in being a member, often generate conflict. Conflict situations frequently arise within communities of belief and identification, for example in religious communities. This can occur less often within communities of interest, such as communities of stamp and coin collectors. Members come to be at odds with other members, and within themselves, because they possess conflicting commitments. Often this situation occurs when one element of a community insists that all aspects of the subculture (or sub-subculture) be observed and followed. Such adherence often requires that ties to all other communities be cut—including families of origin, creation, affiliation, and so forth. Such groups may be considered fundamentalist and totalitarian, and their members may be termed "zealots" or "true believers."

## STAGES OF COMMUNITY GROWTH

Social units—families, groups of people, organizations, or societies—exist in different phases of growth, maturity, decline, and renewal. Different problems are generally associated with each phase. The community social worker should be aware of these phases as part of an overall awareness of community issues and difficulties, though entire communities cannot be easily typed. Some, for example, contain both growing and declining sections. Others have conflicting components—a young population in a very old geographic area. Many other combinations present themselves when we examine stages of community growth.

### Young Communities

New communities tend to have the problems associated with youth everywhere: lack of control and resources. Young communities often grow in a haphazard fashion. In a neighborhood community for example, there may be an absence of regulation or structure that focuses the community on where to place what kind of facility, and so on. Community development workers may need to assist in developing such processes and structures.

Resource problems are another typical difficulty for young communities. Being new, young communities have not had the time to develop information networks and referral centers where individuals can come together and exchange information and help. They may not have had the time to discover which of their members are community leaders and influencers.

Community development workers in young communities try to assist in the creation of community leadership, which, in turn, helps others to identify needed resources and, together with the community development worker, to begin the process of resource development. New communities are typically communities of strangers, and community workers may assist in the development of legitimate mechanisms for interaction and interpersonal contact.

A young community, for example, may be a community of the newly separated and divorced. Community workers may assist in establishing parents-without-partners groups and other places where newly single individuals can meet others, talk with them, and develop patterns of mutually satisfying interaction. Overall, young communities tend to be characterized by the need for community development, followed by community action and community planning. (Although planning can be very useful in young communities, the motivation to plan may be low until the community has matured.)

## Middle-Aged Communities

Middle-aged communities have existed for some time and function reasonably well. In fact, it is this "reasonably well" functioning that creates a problem. Middle-aged communities are often beset by conflict. What kinds of conflicts might be present? Multiple community identifications to geographic locations; work, business, and profession; religious belief; and political interest might be among those competing for the identifications of individual community members.

Community development is useful in such circumstances to blend different identifications and seek to create common purpose. Community action to improve civic facilities is helpful, and planning can help determine and clarify the direction a community should pursue.

A second major problem middle-aged communities face is failure to change. The young community is constantly changing and needs stability and organization; the middle-aged community, however, needs to adjust and improve its houses, local facilities, social structure, and orientation to take account of the changing world around it. Community workers can help middle-aged communities chart the forces acting on them and prepare for action by planning for positive change.

## Old Communities

Older communities are often in need of renewal. Geographic communities are not infrequently characterized by older industries and populace. (Although an older populace does not always indicate the presence of an older community.) Younger individuals may well have left to follow job opportunities in new industry; small rural towns and big cities are frequently found in this category. A sense of depression and inadequacy may pervade an older community. Community ties may exist, but community conflicts may preclude the community from taking action. Therefore, community action to begin the renewal process is a good first step, because community planning cannot proceed without a sense of efficacy.

Older physical communities frequently demonstrate a decline in facility upkeep, and they maintain preexisting, outmoded patterns and forms. The community action worker may seek to revivify and reinstitute some of these elements with the cooperation of local leaders. Additional features associated with an older geographic community include crime and decay. These difficulties provide a good basis for community action. Neighborhood watch programs and other activities crystallize community energy around social activities that are helpful to the community as a whole, and present a good place to begin a renewal process.

Communities that are not geographically based also experience problems of renewal and recruitment. The commitments, feelings, and emotions that promote community identification need to be passed on to newer members and recruits. Sometimes reorganization of the community—establishing different goals, purposes, and emphases—is needed as well. The community worker can help in this renewal process.

## CONCLUSION

Communities, then, assume many different forms, because common elements vary across many dimensions. These dimensions range from geographic, gender, age, affliction, and interests (hunting, fishing) to ethnic origin, religion, college and university affiliation, and workplace, to name just a few. For this reason, we are all members of many communities, some of which we recognize and cherish, others whose existence is unknown to us, and still others that are potential communities.

Of course, each community has its own subculture, with norms and values. There is, therefore, bound to be intra- and intercommunity conflict. Intracommunity conflict can occur, for example, between the more liberal and the more orthodox members of a large religious community (Catholics, Jews, Muslims, and so forth). Much effort goes into processing and managing the competing claims of our communities; sometimes we manage successfully, oftentimes not.

Successful community organization and leadership require workers and citizens to be aware of the many different types of communities, their conflicts, and their stages of social organization and the problems and concerns each stage presents. Young, middle-aged, and old communities have disparate sets of problems and concerns. As you will see in the next chapters, each set requires somewhat different strategies.

# Chapter 2
## Community Problems, Organization, and Leadership

This chapter considers three archetypical community problems or issues and then explores three models of community organizing and leadership. Such models might be orchestrated by a professional community worker, a local community leader, or both working in concert. Sometimes the community worker adopts an informal leadership role at the start of an organization initiative, while simultaneously developing local leaders to whom initiatives can be passed as the worker or organizer moves into a supportive role.

## ARCHETYPICAL COMMUNITY PROBLEMS

*Disorganization* seems to be the overriding problem to which community organization addresses itself. But community disorganization is a vague diagnosis that sounds negative and judgmental. *Unorganization* might be better. Three kinds of unorganization difficulty can serve as a basis for community change and development efforts: lack of community cohesion, lack of community capability, and lack of community competence.

*Cohesion* is the mutual identification that undergirds a community. *Capabilities* refer to a community's ability to translate those mutual identifications into actions. *Competence* is the scope, integration, and overall success of these efforts. Each, in a sense, builds on the other. Without cohesion, neither capability nor competence is possible. Without cohesion and capability, competence is not possible. Let us consider each problem, each possibility for community growth, in turn.

## Issues of Community Cohesion

One of the basic problems a community worker or leader faces is how to develop and build community cohesion. A community that lacks cohesion is in some sense not a community yet. There may be normlessness or *anomie*—a lack of common values in a group—and an absence of mutuality and mutual identification. The community worker selects and proposes projects that will increase community cohesion—that is, projects that promote commonness and projects that aim to develop a perception of common faith and involvement.

A typical cohesion-building project in a geographic community is a paint-up-and-fix-up campaign. The explicit goal is to help the community look sharper, crisper, and cleaner. However, the implicit goal of such a campaign is to involve individuals in common activities, an experience they might not have had in the geographic-community context for quite some time. As individuals work together on the designated paint-up-and-fix-up area, they talk and interact with each other and, it is hoped, they begin to perceive the commonalities so clear to others but as yet hidden from themselves. Encouraging perceptions of commonality can result in the development of community cohesion.

Community workers who involve local leaders in cohesion-building activities may use additional techniques, such as holding a community meeting to discuss common problems. To implement this technique, the community worker may use the *critical incident method*. Specifically, the worker meets informally, one-on-one with members of the community. When an incident occurs that stimulates community interest and activity—a crime or victimization, perhaps—the worker proposes a community meeting. Community members may be willing to come together to discuss the fairly simple issue of what to do about this particular incident. This response begins the process of mutual identification that might lead to other types of community development activity.

Workers focused on community cohesion endeavor to "start where the client is" and involve community members in issues and concerns that represent visible community problems. As community members develop interaction with one another, the community worker and community members might consider addressing problems of a broader scope.

A typical beginning place is a block club. Community workers may get people together who live on the same block. (For our purposes, a block consists of those houses facing each other on either side of a single street.) Community workers frequently note that individuals on such blocks do not know much about each other; or, even if they are acquainted, they lack a sense of empowerment and ability to deal with common concerns.

Sometimes the community worker builds community cohesion by developing citizens' advisory groups, which are based on local neighborhood institutions. Establishing a community nursing home council is one example. Nursing homes are organizations that are often cut off from the geographic community in which they are located. Founding a citizens' advisory group that provides volunteer services to the nursing home, increases community traffic into and out of the nursing home, and facilitates interaction between the nursing home community and the geographic community is the kind of community development activity that builds community cohesion.

Thus, the nursing home council (or school–community council or any other kind of organization–community link) serves at least a double purpose. First, it assists the local organization in linking with the geographic community. Second, it influences the organization to act and behave in ways that are helpful to the geographic community and reflect geographic community preferences and interests. When community members talk with organizational representatives and exchange views, they build community cohesion. The advisory council might also be stimulated by an organizational change social worker assisting the organization, in cooperation with a community worker assisting the geographic community or those interested in helping it.

The development of community cohesion always has two goals, a task goal and a process goal. The *task goal* refers to the specific effort or change that the community is striving toward; its achievement is task achievement. A *process goal* refers to the increase in community confidence caused by successful community change and improvement efforts. Thus, at one level, community workers encourage a string of specific community achievements. At another level, they strengthen the community's capacity for capable action, which arises from achievement.

## Issues of Community Capability

A community lacks capability when it is cohesive but lacks a vehicle or organization through which to effectively act. For example, members of a block club may know each other, but it may not occur to them to organize and influence the events that affect them. In this case, the community worker might seek to build a block club federation of representatives from block clubs scattered throughout a geographic community.

Or, the community worker might seek to build a neighborhood association or neighborhood service center. In this case, individuals interested in improving the neighborhood might form an improvement association that is not specifically linked to block club organization. The community worker might connect with other community workers and organizational social workers serving the community to develop a "settlement-house" operation that could serve as a focal point for community activities.

Whatever tool or technique a community worker uses, the goal remains the same: to build on existing common bonds in ways that give community members the experience of influencing their environment. Community members may influence their surroundings by meeting with a local organization and persuading it to change a practice or meeting with citywide organizations to request greater neighborhood representation in subunits that serve the neighborhood. For example, African American communities like to have a high representation of African American police officers and firefighters in their neighborhoods. Actions that encourage citywide administration to make this change will build community capability. Community social work seeks to develop the capacity of the community to carry out its wishes and desires.

## Issues of Community Competence

If a community is cohesive and capable, it may nevertheless face a lack of competence. *Community competence* is the ability of a local community to act effectively over a period of time. Some communities are able, in a specific situation and for a relatively short time, to take capable action, to exercise influence that benefits the community. But frequently the motivation or spirit making this effort possible fades, and the community is no longer characterized by capability.

A community also lacks competence when it seeks to act but fails to "get together," or does act but fails to secure results. In such cases, the community worker might aim to increase community competence. Because competence is measured over time, the community worker gives special attention to developing local community leadership. Of course, leadership development has been a goal during cohesion and capability efforts. In these phases the community worker inevitably acts in an initiator role, performing more tasks than she or he would in the competence-building phase. These tasks are undertaken on behalf of the community, but the worker works with community members in these particular tasks, as a way of fostering leadership development.

As communities develop and begin to focus on sustained competence, local leadership is vital. Thus, a worker may link community members with city- or statewide leadership development programs. Sometimes schools offer leadership development and social change programs as part of public school or community college activities. Alternately, the community worker can connect with others in the community to develop an independent leadership development program. Regardless of the mechanism used to foster community leadership, community continuity will not remain viable and community competence will decrease without it. Most community workers find that communities have serious, ongoing needs. Thus, the worker endeavors to partner with and involve members of the community so that they can carry on community activities independently.

Community leadership development, as part of community competence building, focuses not only on specific community members, but also on the growth of community groups and community organizations. It is necessary for a community's component organizations to be reasonably viable. Hence, a community worker fosters leadership that may both serve neighborhoodwide or communitywide organizations and may assume leadership roles in organizations that serve the community. As leaders emerge, the community worker may seek to establish a community leadership council, in which leaders from different organizations within the community meet to coordinate efforts, exchange information, and share perspectives.

## THREE APPROACHES TO ORGANIZING
## AND LEADING COMMUNITY CHANGE

How does one help communities to move toward positive change? Though many approaches exist, a threefold model provides a useful overall framework for planning positive change (see Table 2-1). The framework is based on a problem that a community faces. Sometimes common features are present, but individuals neither perceive them as common nor recognize the bonds that could arise from recognizing them. Here, community development will help citizens recognize and gain strength from their commonality. A second problem occurs when a community recognizes common features and fate but seems unable to galvanize its latent energy and take purposeful steps to advance its own interests. In this case, community action is called for. A third problem emerges when people experience multiple community identifications. Such multiplicity of communal involvements can lead to community conflicts (for example, between black and white communities, Jewish and Catholic communities, work and geographic communities) and may forestall the potential for action. Such a case is a good reason to draw on community-planning resources.

### Community Development

Community development activities are those that promote recognition of common features and lead to interaction based on those features (Lowe, 1995; Rothman, Erlich, & Tropman, 1995; Spergel, 1987). Community development typically involves the community worker taking initiative, talking with potential members of a community, assessing the extent of their nascent recognition of possible links with others and their willingness to talk with others who share a common feature. For example, a community worker might talk with several individuals on a particular block to assess their willingness to get together with others on the block to discuss issues of common concern. A community worker might talk with women who have experienced assault to see whether they would be interested in connecting with other victims to explore common interests and concerns. In a remote village, a community worker might begin partnering with local chiefs and opinion leaders to encourage village members to focus on some common task.

## TABLE 2-1: Three-Model Framework of Approaches to Community Change

| DEVELOPMENT | ACTION | PLANNING |
| --- | --- | --- |
| High-involvement projects | Organizing functional communities (these are communities of identification—the Jewish community, for example—but there is an injustice element involved in the organizing) | Social planning (using technical means—data, equations, projections—to forecast the future and making recommendations on the basis of that work) |
| Neighborhood organizing (getting folks together) | Political action (pressuring local officials, state officials for redress; using the legal system to make change) | Program development (working to bring about technical improvements in service delivery) |
| Program development (getting folks together around some project or program, e.g., a school fair or a paint-up, fix-up campaign) | Social action (using public means, such as protest marches, public demonstrations, and the like to heighten general awareness of both participants and observers; it often involves "rubbing raw the sores of discontent") | Community liaison (central planners—governmental or voluntary—seeking to establish relationships with local planning and action groups) |
| Community social and economic development (using local participation to develop businesses and firms, which in turn creates jobs) | Propaganda of the deed (using TV and radio to publicize injustices as a way to get airtime; it usually takes advantage of some newsworthy event) | Environmental planning (technical planning, which often involves land use, development, water, waste, and so on) |
| Community education (sharing information in group settings—on HIV/AIDS, for example) | | Health planning (technical planning centered around health concerns and issues) |
| | | Physical planning (technical planning centered around spatial design) |
| | | Coalitions (building relationships with other organizations to work in concert) |

This is *consciousness raising*—a phrase with origins in the feminist movement—the process by which common features, qualities, or fates that bind individuals together but have hitherto been unrecognized or acted on are brought to the surface. One fairly dramatic communal development, and a new one, is the emergence of the Adult Children of Alcoholics (ACOA) group (Black, 1981). Children who grew up in a home where a parent was an alcoholic, or otherwise emotionally impaired, share common experiences with thousands of others. Although this commonality was present, it remained latent, unrecognized until the late 1970s. Now, there are ACOA chapters around the country. Members get together, share common experiences, and make plans for common action. They even hold a national conference. This emergence of commonality is a perfect example of community development.

## Community Action

Sometimes a community recognizes itself as sharing common features or fate but is unable to mobilize itself to press its needs, requests, or demands (Burghardt, 2001; Rothman et al., 1995). Here the community worker may seek to assist a group in undertaking community, or social, action. *Community action* refers to that set of activities that places pressure on decision makers to prevent exploitation, improve social conditions, or increase benefits. It is typically deployed when improvements are needed in a community and when the community and its members are victims of crime, social injustice, and exploitation. It can involve mass mobilization, leader influence, or both. It can be based on geographic features, common interest, common fate, or common beliefs (Bell, 1995).

The recent public employees union movement provides a good case study of community action. In early 2011, the governor of Wisconsin proposed an end to collective bargaining rights for state workers. The members of the state workers' union took action in the form of mass mobilization and lead influence. Their needs involved better working conditions, better wages, greater job stability, and the development of an effective organized force that could act on par with the organized force of management organization. There was great resistance to formal union organization in its initial stages, as is often the case with community action efforts. (Dominant forces often seek to delegitimatize, deemphasize, and destabilize community action efforts to retain the advantages they enjoy.) But with assistance and persistence, community action can be successful. In this instance, state workers' union community action spread across the country.

The work of the Gray Panthers and the American Association of Retired Persons provides another example of broad community action. Older adults comprise a larger proportion of society, are concentrated in specific geographic areas, and have a high propensity to vote. Thus, they have become an increasingly political force that can take effective community action. Community workers at senior citizens centers around the country seek to bring together older adults and assist them in talking with each other about matters of common concern, such as the cost of health care, Medicare benefits, and social security benefits. From these discussions emerge letter-writing campaigns, political influence campaigns, and senior days in state capitols (organized events in which older adults come to meet with legislators and communicate the needs of the older population).

Community or social action is also evident in victims' rights activities. These individuals, concerned that more attention has been spent on the perpetrator than the victim, draw attention to victims' rights by bringing victims together so that they can develop common perspectives. Victim action activities have included pressing (and witnessing the passage of) legislation that ensures victim compensation, victim testimony during sentencing and parole hearings, and victim advocate officers in local jurisdictions.

Sometimes community action involves mass demonstrations. The 1963 March on Washington for Jobs and Freedom, spearheaded by Martin Luther King, Jr., is one such example. The well-known community activist, Saul David Alinsky, often used this method of social action, trying to highlight individuals' incongruities and conflicting commitments by picketing slum landlords as they left church or inviting all residents of a particular neighborhood to capture and kill a rat and deposit it on the steps of city hall (Alinsky, 1946, 1971, 1992; Bailey, 1976). Sit-ins have also become a popular form of mass activity. Social action also involves use of the influence of elite connections, as when community influentials seek—through small meetings and informal interaction—to influence key decision makers on a one-on-one basis.

Community Planning

Because communities differ, it is sometimes the case that the demands of one community are opposed to the demands of another (Gummer, 1995; Rothman et al., 1995). Thus, community conflict may result, or a person may be unable to act because the demand of one community cancels out the imperatives of the other. A community's interests frequently stem from the one or two features its members hold in common, and it may have no broader view that takes into account the range of interests that may characterize, perhaps, a large city or county area. Community planning is useful in such a complex situation; community workers use knowledge, research, and information, as well as the involvement of the several different groups concerned with the future of a particular issue or area, to develop and implement ideas that benefit all concerned (Vinter & Tropman, 1971).

Whereas community development and community action tend to be participative—directly involving as many community members as possible—community planning tends to be representative and proceeds by participation of delegates. It is not possible to have all members of the Jewish community, the African American community, the gay community, the various geographic communities, and so on, meet together; thus, representatives are a logical choice. The community plan solicits the participation of influential representatives from various communities working together on some larger community committee or task force. Planning decisions that a group of relative elite (or opinion leaders) make have a greater chance of acceptance among specific component communities (Tropman, 1971).

Community planning relies heavily on information and interaction around information. Environmental scans and needs assessments provide information about impending pressures and problems. Social analyses offer a picture of how current difficulties and problems are distributed (Davis & Botkin, 1994).

Technique exchange and program sharing among community planners provide one source of ideas about how to approach problems. A second source is the particular multicommunity group convened to discuss an issue or issues. These issues of fact and value are addressed in the committee or group meeting and, over time, the community planner seeks to achieve an agreement among representatives of different interests and communities for a course of action.

By processing information through representative groups, the ideas and feelings of the broader groups can be taken into account. Criticisms of this approach, however, center on the extent of representation and the possibility of *cooptation,* which occurs when members of the community or study group in question forget the interests of their groups of origin.

Finally, community planning tends to be more professional and technical than other approaches to community involvement and change. This level of, or approach to, community involvement and change has the potential to erode community cohesion. Such a loss can, in turn, undermine the vitality of community competence. Thus, the community worker and leader must be mindful about issues of development. The growth of a community is a complete circle.

### Other Approaches to Community Change

The three-model approach, useful as it is, is giving way to a multiple-model approach (Weil & Gamble, 1995). Thus, it is better to regard the three models discussed above as a template under which more specific approaches can be developed, or as a good organizing framework within which to consider the many specific tactics used in current community work.

## PROBLEMS EXIST TOGETHER AND OVERLAP

The three problems discussed earlier—cohesion, capability, and competence—exist, to a great degree, simultaneously. It is difficult for the community worker to make an accurate diagnosis about where in the cycle of growth the community is, so that effective beginning efforts can be made. In some sense, the community worker will make a simultaneous effort to strengthen cohesion, capability, and competence.

One way to think about this simultaneousness is to envision three overlapping circles. Each represents one problem: cohesion, capability, or competence. Sometimes, of course, an issue exists by itself. At other times two exist together. The center, where the three circles overlap, represents a situation in which all three problems exist at once.

Efforts to strengthen community cohesion tend to draw on community development skills; efforts to improve community capability tend to draw on community action skills; building community competence involves community planning. Most community workers find that—although these distinctions can be made for the sake of discussion—in the actual work of community change, development, action, and planning are often simultaneous efforts.

## CONCLUSION

Three issues and three models is an oversimplification of the complex mosaic of community organization and leadership. The three sets of issues—community cohesion, community capability, and community competence call attention to three *nodes*, or specific areas, of concern.

And the three interventions do capture three overarching streams. Development creates connection and the awareness of connection. Action advocates for social justice against entrenched powerful interests. Planning takes up the more technical aspects of anticipating the future and the steps needed to get there. None exist alone; each requires the others; when one is identified, it is actually its prominence that is being noted. Community organizers and leaders need to be aware of the three signature problems and three signature approaches to addressing them.

Community change involves enhancing, developing, and strengthening the commonly held bonds that people have with each other. Much that is possible through community effort is not possible by individual effort alone. Much of what happens to individuals depends on the community in which they live and the strength and vigor of that community. Yet it is also true that individuals sometime fail to recognize the common unity that they share; or, if they recognize it, they fail to act on it or fail to act effectively and efficiently. Community development helps people recognize and understand commonalities.

Community action seeks to enable individual communities to take specific steps to advance their own interests. Such steps often involve "carefrontation" of one sort or another—frequently against entrenched power interests who benefit from the status quo. Slum landlords, for example, have little interest in improving the quality of their housing stock.

Community planning seeks to regularize and institutionalize community influence efforts by establishing longer-range goals and a broader representation of community participants. In all these efforts, the community worker and local community leader play a vital role.

Each problem and approach occur in a sort of order. Difficulties in community cohesion, which are often addressed through community development initiatives, tend to appear in young communities. Communities struggling with capability, typically approached with community action tactics, tend to be middle-aged communities. Difficulty sustaining community competence, addressed with community planning strategies, often appear in mature communities.

Although problems and approaches do occur together, efforts at change need to build on one another. First, community cohesion needs to be enhanced, or capability will not be very successful. When capability is attended to, the community builds experience of efficacy and success. And finally, community competence is enhanced, building on and burnishing capability.

Within that rough progression exists a sense of priority. For one thing, components of a community may be at different stages; thus, different approaches may be required among different elements simultaneously. In addition, each phase is undertaken with an eye to the succeeding phase, much as in eight-ball pool a player seeks to sink an opponent's ball *and* position the cue for the next shot.

# Chapter 3

## Phases, Competencies, and Goals in Community Organization and Leadership

A s in most helping and intervention efforts, the community worker proceeds through phases as the process of help develops. There is a beginning, middle, and ending phase. In the real world of community development, action, and planning, things do not always proceed as neatly as this description implies, but it does represent a perspective from which the worker seeks to act, and it does alert the worker to elements that might be overlooked in quickly developing community work.

### PHASES OF HELPING

#### Beginning Phase

In the beginning phase, community workers endeavor to recognize and define a problem, then assess information pertaining to it. This process does not always follow the tidy order implied. Most desirable, of course, would be for the community worker to collaborate with individuals in a particular community area and for them to recognize that a problem exists.

Problem recognition can occur on many levels. Community cohesion is a theoretical way to define a community problem. It is unlikely that community members would identify a problem as lack of community cohesion (or lack of community capability or competence, for that matter). But they might say something like, "Nobody knows each other around here." "We seem to be a lot of strangers." "With people moving in and out so much, it's hard to find out what's going on." Statements like this indicate a problem of cohesion, and the worker can begin to think through with community members the kinds of things that might make life easier with respect to this particular recognized problem.

However, problem recognition does not necessarily imply problem definition. As a community worker develops an intervention, he or she will need to invest increasing effort on problem definition. The statement, "Nobody around here knows anyone very much," expresses a result condition, but factors contributing to that condition are unclear. Perhaps it is a region of high geographic mobility, or a multicultural or -ethnic area in which individuals from subethnic groups hesitate to cross ethnic or racial boundaries. Perhaps the work schedules of individuals involved in a local community are staggered; hence, only a few people are available at any particular time. Problem definition seeks to focus and identify the causes of particular community problems.

Information gathering assembles factual information based on the problem definition. Sometimes these facts do not support the assumptions of cause that are implicit in the problem definition, and the definition needs to be changed. In other cases, information gathering provides firm and rich evidence to support community beliefs.

Problems of capability and competence also appear in the beginning phase of helping. For example, the community worker may be told, "The city is messing with us" or "The landlords aren't painting and fixing up their buildings, and are gouging people." Such problems suggest an absence of capability and a need for community action activities. Or members of the community might complain that there is a lack of coordination among the agencies and services offered to the community, and more work needs to be done here. Such a problem could suggest difficulties in community competence and the need for planning.

As a practical matter, workers may start at any point in the recognition, definition, and needs assessment process. Sometimes needs assessment is completed first to provide a basis for problem recognition. At other times, community members will assert that they have "recognized" a particular problem. (A new patient may also say to a doctor, "I have disease X.") A worker may withhold judgment on this diagnosis until exploring the views of others and completing a needs assessment. However, even if an initial definition is wrong, it still provides a basis for connecting with community members, and it can become a jumping off place for other efforts.

Needs assessments can range from simple to complicated activities. (See, for example, the very simple "Keep, Stop, Start" model in chapter 13.) At the simplest level, the worker may assemble information drawn from informal discussions with community members and test conclusions from these discussions in community meetings. Often, though, more detailed and factual needs assessments are needed. In such cases, the worker might use published statistics about crime, infant mortality, and unemployment in the neighborhood, or about the behavior pattern of landlords, the number of rat bites, and so on, to provide a set of specific and empirical bases for community discussion. At a still more complicated level, the worker may connect with university researchers or others to approach an actual sample of the community with a detailed community questionnaire. These data may also be linked with published data based on the community in question, and they may present a fairly detailed and scientific picture of community needs.

As in most areas of community development work, the needs assessment in the beginning phase serves a dual purpose. It is designed, in part, to generate information. But the community worker would make a mistake if she or he believed that was its sole purpose and that its concerns were only technical. Developing community information presents an excellent opportunity to involve community members in activities that concern the community. Hence, efforts should always be made to bring in local community members as part of the needs assessment process.

In the more simple needs assessment, not only should the worker talk with community members, but community members should also do so, volunteering their time to flesh out the information picture by interviewing their neighbors and friends. As community statistics are needed from city and other commercial sources, community volunteers can participate in the development of these statistics.

If the project becomes technical and requires university and other professionals, community members can serve in an advisory capacity and can be trained as interviewers to follow the specific scientific needs of a particular survey. During this (and any) activity, the community worker remains sensitive to both process and task needs. Many needs assessment efforts have gone awry because—though technically wonderful—they were done by people outside the community and involved no one in the community. Their impact was limited; sometimes they even generated hostility and were counterproductive.

### Middle Phase

In the middle phase of helping in a community, emphasis is placed on goal selection, prioritization, and goal achievement. By the time the beginning phase draws to a close and the middle phase begins, community members will have suggested a number of possible action steps. This is the moment for goal selection. In some instances, goals have already been selected. Frequently, the process of discussing goal alternatives points, almost automatically, to the clear selection or desirability of one particular goal over others.

In other instances, there may be competing interests and perspectives with regard to goal selection. The worker needs to continue to interact with and encourage community members as they work through the process of selecting a goal and prioritizing the efforts needed to get to that goal. For some communities, setting the goal of goal selection is the achievement of a major process goal.

Some communities are unable to crystallize their efforts around any particular goal, and their efforts remain forever diffuse. (Social workers will recognize that individuals have this same problem. In individual work with a particular affected client, a social worker may seek to help the individual outline possible alternatives, specify the consequences, and work through the problems of picking one for initial focus.)

During the process of goal selection and review, the community worker attends many community meetings. Some take place with large groups of community members, some may be on specific blocks, and some involve an individual leader or small group of leaders. In all cases, participants consider the issues involved, elicit the feelings and perspectives of the group, and involve as many community members as possible in the review process.

At times, the worker should collaborate with community leaders to establish a community decision instrument. It is frequently unclear what person or group should make a decision for the community. Sometimes it is possible to get everyone together in a sort of "old New England town meeting." At other times, coalitions of existing community groups and agencies need to be assembled. The process of community decision making is often vague—not only regarding who should be involved, but also with respect to the mechanism by which the final decision is made.

As a community moves toward a decision, the community worker plays both an encouraging and a supporting role. He or she helps a decision to emerge and raises questions and concerns about particular courses of action. This technique ensures that participants have taken all implications into consideration. For example, a community may quickly select a particular landlord to pressure for repairs on his buildings. The worker may diplomatically raise with the community decision makers the fact that the landlord lives in another state and that putting pressure on the landlord as a first step in community action may be problematic.

"Perhaps," the worker may suggest, "selecting a couple of local landlords as a first step might make more sense." The worker would never attempt to force her or his views on the community. But community workers, like all social workers, must continually work with clients and client systems to help them understand the effects of the actions they are contemplating.

At this discussion stage, too, the worker raises questions about specific steps required to implement a decision. If a community plans a paint-up-and-fix-up campaign, is a community committee in charge of the event? If so, who will serve on that committee and what resources will they need? If resources are needed, how will they be procured? The worker stands ready to assist the community in carrying out goals it sets. However, she or he takes care not to become a default decision maker or to become overinvolved in implementing steps toward a goal rather than encouraging volunteer efforts of community members. The community worker must always remember that the goal belongs to the community and, therefore, community members must take primary responsibility for implementing it.

## Ending Phase

The ending phase contains two subparts—operation; then, assessment, recycle, and termination. *Operation* occurs when community members implement the actual activities decided on during goal selection. If a community planning effort is to be undertaken, the technical aspects of community planning occur here. (Though the whole process of goal development and selection is also a part of community planning.) The worker assists the community in carrying out the plan and may participate in, for example, a paint-up-and-fix-up day, a needs assessment, or another event, provided worker participation does not minimize community participation. The worker joins with, but does not replace, community effort.

Achieving program or goal implementation is always a high point for the community and, to a certain extent, the worker. It is frequently the result of months or even years of community change effort. The successful completion of a particular community change process is gratifying to everyone. However, this gratification presents a problem because the process has not actually ended. During the operation phase, the worker may suggest ways to evaluate the particular change effort and ask how the momentum and enthusiasm developed by a particular project can be later channeled to other goals and projects, perhaps some on a goal priority list. A community that is tightly focused on achieving a particular goal may not be very interested in assessment. Still, it is the worker's professional responsibility to initiate consideration of next steps, just as a physician who, in working with a patient, gives attention to the critical phase of an illness and also talks with the patient about such issues as nutrition and lifestyle that the patient will encounter after moving through the critical phase of illness.

*Assessments* may range from simple debriefings of those involved in a particular meeting or change effort to reasonably complex numerical and statistical presentations about effect, percentage of change, and so on. It is important for the worker to encourage consideration of assessment during the implementation stage because certain assessment activities should take place at the same time as implementation. Although assessment occurs after implementation, thought about assessment design begins early in the interaction process.

Working through an assessment process is often an effective way to initiate recycling. *Recycling* channels the energy developed by one successful community intervention to the next community goals on a priority list. All too frequently, positive feelings and community energy generated by successful goal achievement dissipate, and the worker needs to begin again.

At this point, *termination,* the end of a worker's relationship with a particular community, sometimes occurs. Community workers are in short supply; community needs are high. Workers can seldom spend an entire career in one community. It is hoped, as with an individual or organizational client, that once the community completes a successful cycle of development, it will be able, using its own developed leadership, to continue the practices just completed. Workers often prepare for a transition by discussing with community members the workers' need to move to other communities. Indeed, termination frequently depends on factors other than the community's development cycle. For example, worker funding is often a deciding factor. If the worker is a student, the school year may also exert its own influence. Whenever termination occurs, the worker engages the community and endeavors to help it establish mechanisms for continued involvement and development.

## COMPETENCIES IN COMMUNITY CHANGE

*Competence* is the presence of knowledge, plus skill in applying that knowledge. Two elements are required in a community change effort, regardless of where the community is in its life cycle, what problem needs to be addressed, what model or approach the worker is using, or what phase the work is in. Intellectual and interpersonal competence are indispensable requirements for successful change. Intellectual and interpersonal elements are both goals of community change efforts and means to goal achievement. At times, one becomes the goal, and the other becomes the means. Let's consider each facet of competence in turn.

### Intellectual Competence

Intellectual competence refers to the conceptual knowledge and skills (the ability to apply knowledge) community workers or organizers have. Several kinds of knowledge are needed when working with a community. Workers should be informed about the social science of communities and the forces that shape and change them both generally and within specific social and cultural contexts. They should attend to cultural differences:

Minority communities will differ from majority communities; urban neighborhoods from rural villages. Workers need to know what forces affect communities in common and which are unique to particular settings, and they need to know where to get this information. Community workers also need to know about the steps in the community change processes and the problems that might occur at any specific stage. (These stages are discussed in chapters 1 and 2.)

Community workers need diagnostic skills and the ability to analyze a community situation and understand which of the many elements at play are crucial to community health and which are less central. Synthesis, too, is vital. It is the ability to analyze diverse views and positions and determine what commonalities might lie beneath the surface (Tropman, 1995). Among other knowledge and skills, community workers need to know about and be able to implement assessment, decision processing, decision management, and group process.

As stated earlier, intellectual competence is more than just knowledge. It is the ability to deploy that knowledge appropriately and effectively. The community worker must know how to apply and blend theories and research into practical on-the-ground suggestions. To some extent, this translation process—transferring "what I know" into "how I act"— distinguishes book-smart workers and leaders from effective ones.

There is, of course, no definitive list of knowledge and skills that organizers should master, so constant study and development are necessary. Much material is available about community organization and leadership, so a regular program of reading and discussing with peers and mentors would be helpful. On the skills side, practicing the knowledge gleaned and reflecting on that practice are essential to growing as an effective community worker.

## Interpersonal Competence

Community workers need to be *emotionally* or *relationally intelligent*. This means they need to understand the social science of human behavior and weave that knowledge into how they present themselves in social interaction.

Community members need to establish a relationship with the worker to develop open communication. Just as in more interpersonal modes of practice, community workers must have a level of self-knowledge that allows them to examine the ways they interact with community members, so that good relationships can be developed. Workers may need to present themselves differently when working in differing communities.

For example, in community planning efforts, the worker may use more technical aspects of his or her skills than would be true in community development or community action initiatives. Working with elite members of a community may require different presentations of self than those required when working with other members of the same community. Working with affluent members of a community may require approaches and interactions different from those appropriate when working with disadvantaged members. Dress, language, and style of interaction may all change depending on the nature of the community. The important point is that the community worker be aware of the need for differential presentations of self, assess the type of self-presentation that would be helpful in a particular interaction, and decide on what presentation to offer. Of course, understanding and relating well to others means understanding oneself as well (Burghardt, 2001).

## TASK AND PROCESS GOALS

In each of the models, problem types, and phases, both task goals and process goals are intertwined. But, generally, *task goals* are specific, often structural, outcomes or quantifiable goals: completing a report, planning an event, coming to a decision about an item, completing a clean-up-and-fix-up community day, and so on. *Process goals* generally focus on such aims as building and enhancing relationships; it may not be as simple to determine when they have been achieved. A balance is always necessary. Too much task orientation strains relationships, and too much process focus inhibits accomplishment.

## CONCLUSION

Community work—community organizing and leadership—moves forward in phases. It has a beginning, middle, and end. Of course, there may be subcycles within a larger community cycle; some components of the community may be at the beginning, whereas others are nearer the end. Both intellectual and interpersonal competencies are needed to both recognize and harmonize the smaller cycles within the larger community framework. As community workers progress through the cycles within the community they are serving, they alternate emphasis on broad tasks and process goals, as well as the specific tasks and process goals that are needed within each cycle.

# Part Two
## Taking Leadership in Community Groups

Alexis de Tocqueville (1841) pointed out in *Democracy in America* that America's backbone is the association and gathering of citizens to pursue personal and social good. This motivation for personal and social good has been, and remains, a significant component of American culture.

Such associations do not function automatically; rather, they are opportunities for citizen leaders to offer guidance. Community organization and leadership is largely expressed through such organizations. The nature of such associations varies widely; they include, but are not limited to, civic groups, action groups, boards of voluntary agencies, neighborhood groups, interest groups (animal helping and animal rights, fishing, stamp and coin clubs), and self-help groups.

And, as discussed in chapter 1, communities take many forms. They can exist geographically—at the block, neighborhood, town, regional, state, national, and international levels. They can exist within organizations or among organizations. Consider, for example, a social workers group at the University of Michigan and a social workers group from colleges across the country. Communities can exist among people with a certain affinity, such as the Log Cabin Republicans, a Republican organization "dedicated to representing the interests of gay and lesbian Americans and their allies" (Log Cabin Republicans, 2011).

What is the work of a community? It consists of both task and process elements. In terms of task elements, it creates outcomes. In terms of process elements, it encourages diverse constituents and stakeholders to participate in determining what outcomes to pursue, and it balances the competing values that inevitably emerge. It is through this latticework of groups and their interconnections that associations and organizations—communities—do their work.

Such associations often need assistance. Sometimes community workers assist the community with issues of cohesion, recognizing their common bonds. They may help a cohesive community become capable, better at what it does. Or, they may assist capable communities in becoming better at community work, striving toward competent community decision making.

Community organization and leadership is a role that both citizens and professionals can play. Part 2 of this book attends to defining leadership roles, examining how to address common problems, clarifying the jobs of group chairpeople and members, and discussing the responsibilities of groups. It contains eight chapters. Chapter 4 considers obstacles to working together in communities. It also provides some guidelines for helping community work to succeed. Chapters 5, 6, and 7 deal with community committees, a common structure through which community leadership and organizing gets accomplished. Chapter 5 addresses community committee responsibilities, chapter 6 focuses on the chairperson, and chapter 7 considers the members' responsibilities. Chapter 8 looks at the different roles and responsibilities of the community leader or chairperson.

# Chapter 4

## Obstacles to and Guidelines for Working Together in Community Development

Community enhancement brings people together to improve their lives and opportunities. Although every individual has his or her own interests, each of us also acts on behalf of the entire community, expressing a trustee or stewardship function for the whole rather than just our part. Community organization and leadership assists us in creating both social and personal value for the whole. Almost always, stewardship involves community decision making. This chapter discusses both obstacles to and ground rules for successful community decision making.

Many barriers exist to achieving high-quality decisions that advance the interests of the community as a whole. Some of these complications result from conflict that extends over lifetimes and even generations. Sociologist William Gamson (1966) explores such drawn-out conflicts in *Rancorous Conflict in Community Politics*. Many other conflicts, though, are less complicated, less entrenched, and more easily resolved. However, if not attended to, minor problems can derail the community decision-making process. Community organizers and leaders should be aware of three types of problems: problems of procedure, problems of process, and problems of people.

### PROBLEMS OF PROCEDURE

Sometimes a community group has not established procedures that involve all stakeholders, a cause of several problems, two of which are worth noting here.

## Iron Law of Oligarchy

Political analyst Robert Michels (1949) proposed that, over time, groups tend to be run by a small elite—an oligarchy. This danger always lurks in community leadership, because the small elite enjoys its power. The political groups Michels wrote about were socialist in orientation, striving for a more egalitarian society. However, equality and participation cannot be brought about by exclusion and elitism. Group procedures should ensure that all members of the group take turns at leadership.

## Single-Issue Individualism

American society is individualistic (Riesman, 1954). This tendency, paradoxically, affects groups as well. In a community context, single-issue groups want exactly and only what they want, regardless of the effect on others. There is no culture of community for them. Such groups often are the way they are because repeated problems within the community process have eroded trust. Community organizers and leadership should seek to work with these groups as much as possible to rebuild trust.

## PROBLEMS OF PROCESS

Sometimes the decision-making process becomes mired and twisted, and problems arise. Ancient and modern writers have identified several bad results. I mention some of the most famous, and point out that the concepts and techniques discussed later help avoid these adverse outcomes.

## Folly

Barbara Tuchman (1984) developed this idea in the *March of Folly*. Folly occurs when a community picks a bad direction that extends beyond the community just making poor decisions. Other criteria must be met: Other alternatives were available; a clear set of voices articulated these other options; and the poor decisions occurred over time and were not the result of one person's error. She cites the case of the Trojan horse. The Greeks had besieged the city of Troy, and they devised the strategy of constructing a huge wooden horse and hiding an attack team inside. The Greek army then withdrew, leaving the horse at the gates of the city. The Trojans came out to find the horse and debated what to do about it.

Suggestions included burning the horse or throwing it into the sea. The Trojans decided to bring the horse (and the attack team) into the city. After dark, the attack team emerged and opened the city gates to the Greek army, which destroyed Troy. As a community, Troy lacked good decision-making procedures.

Steve Kerr (1975) discusses a second type of folly in his famous article "On the Folly of Rewarding A while Hoping for B." On one hand, a geographic community may hope to woo a "big box" store to its township. On the other, it may engage in cumbersome zoning and planning discussions. Its pokey, prolonged decision process (A) can kill the hoped-for deal (B).

## Group Think

Some conflict is necessary in community organization and leadership work, because differences that never surface work in corrosive, nonpublic ways. *Group think* refers to making agreements under conditions of high cohesion, in which no one wants to disturb the peace (Janis, 1983). Group think frequently occurs when a powerful individual pressures a group to influence a decision. Group members acquiesce, fearful that they might be punished in some way, or simply unwilling to take on that powerful individual. The agreement is false, however; the minute the meeting ends, individuals other than the powerful promoter are usually complaining among themselves. Sabotage may begin right away. Janis identified several components of group think:

- *Incomplete survey of alternatives.* Group limits discussion to a few courses of action without surveying the full range of alternatives.
- *Incomplete survey of objectives.* The group does not survey the objectives to be fulfilled and the values implicated by the choice.
- *Failure to examine the risks of the preferred choice.* The group fails to reexamine the course of action initially preferred by most members; it does not consider nonobvious risks and drawbacks not brought out when it originally evaluated its preferred choice.
- *Failure to reappraise initially rejected alternatives.* The group neglects courses of action initially evaluated as unsatisfactory, spending little or no time discussing whether they have overlooked nonobvious gains.

- *Poor information search.* The group makes little or no attempt to obtain information from experts who can supply sound estimates of gains and losses expected from alternative courses of action.
- *Selective bias in processing information.* The group likes facts that support what the members want to do; it spends time discussing those facts and tends to ignore evidence of a contrary nature.
- *Failure to work out contingency plans.* The group spends little time deliberating how the chosen policy might be hindered by bureaucratic inertia or political sabotage; thus, the group fails to work out contingency plans.

Paying attention to these problems can prevent many elements of group think. But they require vocalization—speaking up. If no one vocalizes an objection, community groups can fall victim to the Abilene paradox.

### Abilene Paradox

The Abilene paradox was developed by Jerry Harvey (1974). It is that all-too-common situation in which everyone does something that no one wanted to do or goes somewhere that no one wanted to go. Harvey tells the story of a group of people in a car without air conditioning, about an hour outside of Abilene, Texas, on a hot day. Somehow, the group decides to go to Abilene for lunch. They travel a long way in an uncomfortable automobile in the blistering heat. The lunch is awful. On the way back, the group discovers that no one actually wanted to go to Abilene for lunch. The Abilene paradox has come to refer to those kinds of community decisions in which no one wanted to make the decision, but everyone somehow fell into it.

### Garbage Can Model of Community Choice

Cohen, March, and Olson (1972) argued that communities have four types of people: problem knowers, problem solvers, resource controllers, and decision makers looking for work. *Problem knowers* understand the problems individuals and the community face. Ministers, doctors, and lawyers are problem knowers. *Problem solvers* are creative individuals who can come up with ideas for solving problems and getting things done. (Problem solving in a community context may be a bit too complete for my taste; I prefer the phrase "problem managing." But that does not change the point here.) They may not, however, know the community's problems. *Resource controllers* control important community resources. They may not have deep knowledge of community problems or good ideas about how to address problems. But they do sign off on money and people, crucial resources for problem solution or management. Finally, *decision makers looking for work* can bring together disparate elements of a community and help them work together. These individuals tend to be a community's influentials, opinion leaders, and elites, whose approval is necessary for solutions to go forward.

Cohen et al.'s (1972) point is that for high-quality decisions to be made, communities must involve each of these four types in the decision-making process, in the same room, at the same time. For the most part, though, they are assembled haphazardly, as if thrown into a garbage can. Community meetings with only a subset of the four types will come up with the wrong issue (no problem knowers); weak and ineffectual solutions (no problem solvers); inadequate resources (no resource controllers); or no overall permission to proceed (no opinion leaders). Thus, in constructing task forces and steering committees, organizers should include all four types of people.

## Defensive Routines

*Defensive routines,* an idea developed by Harvard University's decision analyst Chris Argyris (1985), refers to a group situation in which certain topics are never discussed. Teenage vandalism in a community might be one example; racial affinity clusters outside the high school entrance or in the cafeteria might be another.

Furthermore, "the non-discussability is never discussed either." Thus, the group never explores reasons for topic avoidance or examines solutions. Such routines may come into play in a community decision-making situation, for example, when a powerful member always gets his or her way. Usually the situation festers, poisoning attempts at community problem solving in other areas as well. Finally, some catastrophic event forces a crack in the carapace of silence and all that has been suppressed spills out. By then, though, much damage has been done.

### Rube Goldberg Construction and Occam's Razor

In the Rube Goldberg construction, complexity, great complexity sometimes, results from the community decision-making process. Faulty process often leads to an overabundance of approaches and steps, creating extra work and threatening or intimidating implementation. A decision that is too complicated to work is sure to break down in both expected and unexpected ways. William of Occam, a clergyman who lived in the early fourteenth century, formulated a rule for judging between competing mathematical proofs. Occam's razor, useful in community work, states that simpler was better; the proof with the fewest steps is the winner (Jones, 1952).

### Brute Think

"Brute think" is a term I use to explain the situation in which a group thinks it can bulldoze its way to a solution by "just keeping at it." Instead of bracketing a problem—setting a difficult issue aside—members hammer away at one solution until others will accept almost any proposal, just to get out of the room.

### Zeno's Paradox

Zeno, a Greek philosopher who lived in the fifth century B.C., observed that, if one approaches a wall and covers half the remaining distance with each step, one will never reach the wall. In community decision making, a group may get closer and closer but never actually make a decision. Zeno's paradox is a type of decision-avoidance psychosis.

### Nondecision, or Boiled-Frog Phenomenon

Nondecision occurs when communities allow events to proceed without acting. They thus find themselves, in a sense, dead. I liken this phenomenon to a high school science experiment. Put a frog in a petri dish of water and slowly heat it over a Bunsen burner. The frog eventually boils to death. Why doesn't the frog jump out? The answer lies in the concept of the just-noticeable difference; that is, in many communities, change happens slowly. Community leaders sometimes do not perceive the changes and thus fail to act. However, a community-based strategic planning process project can help a community avoid becoming a boiled frog.

## PROBLEMS OF PEOPLE

Several personality types can hinder the decision-making process. Harvard University economist Amartya Sen (1992) observed that "spoilers" would prefer to lower others' gain than raise their own. Such partisans are unable to set aside their emotional, personal, or stakeholder issues and commitments to view the community as a whole and determine what might be appropriate for it, rather than for themselves. When they do get together, these single-issue individualists fuse into single-issue groups. Whereas zealots or "true believers" are extreme cases (Hoffer, 1951), politicians use every community process to advance themselves, whether they have political aspirations or are engaging in social climbing.

Novices lack the necessary experience and background to function in a community group. They tend to be naive about how process works and are unsure how to facilitate good process. Their goals are well intentioned but, as we all know, the road to hell is paved with good intensions.

It is tempting to remove these individuals from the decision-making process. Paradoxically, even though such individuals are ineffective, attempts to remove them often build sympathy for their cause. Working with them individually can sometimes be an effective solution. But more often, for spoilers and partisans, finding ways to include them in the community coalition is the most productive alternative.

## ELEMENTS OF GOOD COMMUNITY PROCESS

To be successful, the community decision-making process should be characterized by inclusiveness, trustworthiness, viability, validity, and reliability. An inclusive process involves a wide range of people. A trustworthy process is one in which no back-room decisions have overtaken the public process. A viable process is one in which decisions stand up under pressure and do not erode over time—two factors that suggest they are legitimate decisions. A valid process means the right issues—not "fake" ones—are on the table. A reliable process bases its decisions on accurate information.

## GROUND RULES FOR EFFECTIVE DECISION MAKING

Communities frequently form decision-making groups to solve problems. These groups should adopt ground rules for the decision-making process; principles discussed in this section enhance the inclusiveness, trustworthiness, viability; validity, and reliability of such a process.

### Respect People and Ideas

Respect for people is vital. Every person deserves attention and consideration. Group members should listen attentively to every speaker, avoiding negative body language such as scowling, eye-rolling, head-shaking, or other silently effective means of telling the speaker that he or she is not important. At the same time, speakers and presenters must respect the people who are listening by making points succinctly and avoiding repetition.

One aspect of respecting people is respecting their ideas. However, respect does not mean differences cannot be expressed; indeed, respect for ideas implies and requires that those ideas be tested. On the other hand, ideas should not be referred to in scornful terms. Comments like "that's a stupid idea" help no one. Even if one particular idea is not strong, it may spark another idea in someone else that becomes a building block for community progress.

### Resist Decision-Avoidance Psychosis

Make timely decisions. Just as some evidence of losing weight is essential if one is to be motivated to continue a weight-loss program, decision progress is essential for the group to reach its goals. Although progress does not have to occur overnight, the group must periodically come to decisions, advance certain alternatives, forsake other alternatives, and move on. Groups prone to decision-avoidance psychosis—that is, groups that delay making a decision—will lose members' interest, commitment, and participation.

### Honor Time Commitments

In contemporary western culture, time is a crucial resource. Leaders must honor time commitments for meetings if commitment to the entire community development process is to be sustained. This means meetings must start and end on time. Individuals can plan around them—hiring babysitters or making arrangements for coverage at home or work. Dragging out meetings, failing to start on time, or having to meet again to deal with issues that should have been settled at the previous meeting erodes commitment to the larger process. People who are not sure they can depend on the time commitment they have been promised will not attend meetings.

### Respect the Agenda

Members attending a community meeting should receive information ahead of time, think about that information, and prepare to discuss it. Individuals have the right to expect that the energy they have invested in meeting preparation will be honored by focused activity at the meeting. How might you feel if you went to the movie theater to see a much anticipated—and advertised—movie, only to hear the manager say, "Oh, that didn't get much play, so I sent it back. We are running something else tonight."

## CONCLUSION

Everyone who is involved in community development efforts wants them to succeed. Avoiding the obstacles to effective group process is a key element to working effectively in community development efforts, as is setting up appropriate group structures. The different perspectives of all group members must be melded into workable decision making. Solid procedures and process will not produce that result, but they are an important step toward it. Sloppy procedures almost always create more problems than they solve.

# Chapter 5
## Responsibilities of Community Committees

Community decision-making committees have many responsibilities. This chapter broadly sketches two of those responsibilities—member selection and diversity and building trust and empathy.

## MEMBER SELECTION

Members of community decision-making groups should be selected with an eye for inclusion; a variety of perspectives must be present. Several principles should guide member selection.

### Engage Stakeholders

Although it is not possible to have all stakeholders participate in every decision-making group, a broad range is essential to the community decision-making process. In community service, the types of stakeholders range along the continuum of consumers to providers, with many individuals in the middle. Many cross-community goals such as economic development, health planning, and social planning will have a coordinating or steering group with subgroups working on more specific problems. Even in a service subarea, such as HIV/AIDS concerns, varied interests and organizations may need a central place to discuss and work out differences. A steering group will have the broadest cross-section of stakeholders, and work groups will have a more focused stakeholder membership.

### Engage Citizens

In some sense, all citizens can be seen as stakeholders; however, some have perspectives that are broader than, and different from, those of special interests; these views must be presented during the decision-making process. One community model includes a steering committee of more focused citizen or stakeholder involvement that may be subordinate to a large committee of citizens and stakeholders.

### Engage a Range of Ages, Races, and Genders

Because community group members have a variety of interests, diversity of membership by age, race, and gender should be considered. Single-sex groups or groups of one age range or ethnicity that do not represent the broadest scope of membership should be reconstituted with an eye toward broader inclusion.

### Engage a Range of Leadership

A balance should exist between community leaders and community followers. Most communities have influential individuals who often appear in decision-making groups. Their perspectives and experiences are vital; however, followers must be involved as well, because people who have not historically taken leadership roles have perspectives that may be different from, and as valuable as, those of community leaders.


## DIVERSITY BENEFITS AND PROBLEMS

Diversity in composition is a positive attribute for decision-making groups. However, problems can arise when managing diverse groups.

### Representation and Representativeness

One difficult aspect of diverse groups is understanding and working out the differences between representation and representativeness. When social workers discuss stakeholder and citizen involvement, a diversity of race and gender, or power bases, they mean representation—having some differences among perspectives.

However, the issue of representativeness is different. Individuals invited to join in the community process do not necessarily represent or speak authoritatively for the groups of which they are members. For example, a female group member does not speak for all or even some women. An African American member does not speak for or represent some or all African Americans. Social workers should understand that the views of women, African Americans, and others are views of individuals shaped by their backgrounds and informed by their experiences but are not necessarily the views of their groups.

Social workers who want to find out what various community subgroups think should survey that community or assess its needs. To turn to a female group member and ask, "What do the women think on this issue?" is to seek false data and put the individual asked in a position of discomfort. Likewise, members must also see themselves as individuals and not as spokespeople for women, the African American community, or other groups.

### Work Styles

Diversity brings different work styles. Some differences come from group members' jobs or careers. Community volunteers discuss the differences in time pressure between those who have jobs and those who do not. The former often feel more pressure than the latter. Although most individuals have different amounts of time available at different times of the day, week, and year, the amount of time available should not be confused with the amount of time necessary and agreed on. It is this latter block of time that should drive the decision-making process. Thus, the group member who is extremely busy should think through commitments and make appropriate arrangements so that the necessary time is available. Furthermore, the group must honor those arrangements and not expand the time commitments required. Individuals who have fewer time constraints must not let the availability of time be a process driver that excludes contributions of other community members.

Diversity highlights other differences. Some people are brisk and businesslike; others approach decision making in a less deliberate manner. Each type of person may arrive at the same point within the same time frame, but each may irritate the other. Adjustments for such differences are needed. Groups may wish to explore some of these differences using a Meyers-Briggs assessment (Kiersey & Bates, 1984).

Another difference relates to pressure for final action or openness. Some people are psychologically attuned to seek final action or closure. One approach to this phenomenon is the "Zeigarnik effect," the tension to complete a task once it is begun (Deutch, 1968). A Zeigarnik person knows what he or she wants at the supermarket, makes a beeline for that section, buys the product, and leaves the store. Other individuals are more inclined to seek openness. They might know what they want, but as they find it in one supermarket, they wonder whether another supermarket offers better selection, quality, and lower price; they visit three or four supermarkets before making a decision. Each of these personality temperaments tends to annoy individuals with the opposite orientation. Recognition of these differences can soften their effect by bringing differences in style into the open.

## Learning Styles

Part of the community development process is learning, and people have different learning styles. People who learn by reading written material tend to be oriented to the written word. They find reading the most comfortable medium through which to absorb ideas and concepts. Some are more oral than visual in nature. They may be word-oriented but like to hear rather than read the words. For them, a presentation with bulleted lists and summarized concepts is most effective. Some people are visually oriented, but not to words. Instead, they respond to visual representations of information. Graphs, drawings, and other visual summaries are the most effective. Some people prefer to see the big picture laid out, key concepts mentioned here and there, and they fill in the blanks later. Others cannot grasp the big picture without some sense of the surrounding details; they like to build up to larger decisions. Try to give the big-picture person an overview first. Conversely, give the details person some initial details.

## Personal and Community Agendas: Partisans and Statespeople

Everyone has a personal agenda and reasons why he or she became involved in the community process. For example, agencies may feel the need for involvement to protect their own interests; consumers, clients, and customers may feel that their perspectives should determine the direction a community takes. Community volunteer participants are in the complicated position of being both partisan and statespeople. The partisan pursues his or her own ends; the statesperson actively seeks to understand and construct the community view. The statesperson further understands that his or her personal views might not be well served by a community solution, but nevertheless does not lobby overmuch for his or her own perspective. At a minimum, managing such conflicts involves recognizing explicitly that conflict exists. Several steps can be taken to ameliorate or resolve these issues.

*Identify an Inclusive Decision and Seek a Community Solution.* One view of community process is that partisan and statesperson orientations should fight over an issue, with the strongest personality winning. That, however, is not the view of most community work professionals. Community workers seek to identify a solution that incorporates elements from all interests, in which the solution is not driven by one power. Community professionals seek an all-win, rather than an I-win, solution.

*Articulate the Community View and Keep Vocalizing It.* Group management requires self-reflection, repeated articulation of the importance of a community view, and continual testing of individual proposals in the light of a community view.

*Own Your Own Views and Be Candid about Them.* Ethical responsibility requires a participant not to mask his or her own views as community views. This responsibility involves openness to community influence, even if one ultimately retains his or her partisan view (always an option).

In addition, participation in the community decision-making process requires a willingness to step up to the discussion. For example, if social workers as agency executives are thinking of taking a particular action, it might be appropriate and civil to share those intentions with the community group and get feedback and reaction. It is unsettling to return from a community meeting to news that one agency—whose director was sitting at the meeting and said nothing—is taking action that affects other agencies in the group.

*Terms of Sharing.* Establishing terms of sharing in discussion requires an explicit agreement of how members will approach a topic. Individual members can approach the group for advice in at least three ways. An agency director may wish to solicit input from group members. Using a type 1 statement she or he may say, "I have a particular point of view; I would like to hear your reaction. I am not offering my point of view from the perspective of my changing it; I would like to see what you think." Using a type 2 statement she or he might say, "As an agency director, I am tending in direction X. I have not made up my mind and welcome your input. However, I make no promises with respect to what I will do with that input." Using a type 3 statement she or he may say, "As an agency director, I am tending toward direction X. I have not made up my mind, nor has our board; I want to take your wishes into account. Therefore, I am offering to adjust our trajectory toward K once I know what your thinking is. I am not going to ask for your approval of our conclusions from your review; that remains with us. However, I will make certain adjustments and explain to you later at least how I saw those adjustments being made."

## Community Power

There also are aspects to personal and community agendas that have to do with community power or the lack of it. Sometimes, influential individuals display an irritating sense of entitlement or arrogance. This is frequently unintended, but still it comes across to less powerful and less well connected people as arrogance. Although it usually is not necessary to remind powerful community leaders that humility is an important virtue, it might not hurt.

## Geopolitical Differences

Geopolitical differences involve the geographic places people come from and their differences in prevailing attitudes and orientations. Urban and rural backgrounds are common differences; more subtle differences are apparent within each. Urban areas may vary, for example, by ethnic group or neighborhood. Rural areas may differ in local traditions and resident backgrounds. What people in the city may perceive as a community solution may not be the best solution for people in the country, and vice versa. A community view looks at all sets of needs as legitimate and worthy of attention, respects the people and ideas involved in the solutions, and seeks to craft a solution that has appropriate portions addressing the needs of the people in each location.

## BUILDING EMPATHY AND TRUST

Empathy and trust are essential to the successful community decision-making process. Empathy is the sense of proactively understanding, both intellectually and emotionally, others' perspectives. For example, if a woman talks about her own and other women's concerns regarding women's health, other group members must put themselves in her position as far as possible. It is not enough to recognize the viability of that position, although recognizing viability is an important first step. A sense of active sympathy, a sense of "feeling for" and "feeling with," also is needed. For example, "I understand (I think, I hope) where you are coming from on these issues, and I can try to feel as you might feel." Trust must exist in community decision-making procedures.

### Trust in Procedure

Once trust is established, integrity must follow. Trust in procedure means that things are going to go as they have been announced. For example, the group will honor time commitments and follow agendas.

### Trust in Process

Trust in process means that what one sees is what one gets. People must believe the meeting they attend is the real meeting. When backroom activity—secret meetings of some members and powerful agenda makers who often never attend an open meeting—goes on, the community development process is neither authentic nor trustworthy.

### Trust in People

Group members must be able to share their views and feelings without being ridiculed and insulted, without being approached in a sarcastic manner, and without being interrupted. The entire group must see that these norms are maintained. Trust should also extend beyond the meeting room. As the decision-making process proceeds, possibilities may arise that require confidentiality, especially if ideas are preliminary and decisions have not been made. As individuals share exploratory ideas, they need to feel comfortable that others will respect the preliminary nature of the discussions. Members do not want to receive a telephone call after the meeting from some community person who is not a part of the process saying, "I understand this is going to happen, and here's what I think." Inappropriate sharing outside the group produces destructive norms that affect vital processes and causes members not to attend meetings.

It is also important that group members not take advantage of the process to advance their interests by using inside information gained from the group. For example, it is unethical for a wealthy group participant who hears about a business opportunity to use that information and quickly make a personal profit from it.

## CONCLUSION

As individuals enter the community decision-making process, pressures and differences surface. All group participants need to keep these differences in mind and avoid letting them become disruptive to the process of community development.

# Chapter 6
## The Group Chairperson

Serving as a group chairperson is a complicated and problematic job that involves balancing and changing positions and roles. Part of the problem many chairpeople face is that they do not know what to do as chairperson. A chairperson is an executive leader. The executive aspect of the role involves tasks such as running meetings and making sure that decisions reached are implemented. The leadership aspect of the role involves taking leadership and accepting followership, requires being out front and hanging back, and embraces risk-taking while letting others take risks as well. This chapter helps address the uncertainty that surrounds both aspects of the role.

On occasion, the leadership portion and the executive portion experience role conflict. The executive wants to wrap things up, and the leader wants to explore new and different ways of doing things—perhaps, not doing things that have always been done.

### EXECUTIVE RESPONSIBILITIES

#### From Virtuoso to Maestro

The chairperson-designate may have interests to advance and positions to articulate. In that respect, the chairperson-to-be is like a virtuoso violinist who becomes the conductor. When one assumes the role of chairperson, she or he must take a broader, more diplomatic, community-based view. Much like the violinist who becomes a conductor, the member who becomes a chairperson must leave most of his or her partisan interests behind.

## Asking Questions

The chairperson receives added authority from the group members, and thus his or her statements carry more weight As a result, the chairperson who is accustomed to expressing her or his views must assume a quieter role. Statements and contributions should be modulated and phrased more tentatively. Often, a chairperson best approaches topics through questions. Asking questions such as, "What are the implications of this approach?" or "How can we improve this proposal?" will guide the group better than statements. Statements tend to cut off comment and invite rebuttal; questions invite thought and response.

## Following Procedure/Enforcing the Rules

Each group should establish some procedures for its meetings. Once established, it is the chairperson's responsibility to see that those procedures are followed. The chairperson must be prepared for meetings, have and follow the agenda, and follow up on agreements. If the chairperson fulfills his or her responsibilities, then other group members can be expected to follow as well. Community participants look to chairpeople to enforce procedures and rules.

## Managing Difficult People

Chairpeople have to deal with difficult people. For example, when speakers drone on, the chairperson will need to say, "Please wrap up your comments in the interest of time." For the more problematic person—say, someone who is hostile toward others—the chairperson may need to meet with the individual outside the meeting (Bramson, 1981), privately exploring issues and conveying the negative effect that his or her behavior is having on the community group.

Although some individuals are difficult to deal with, many problems with difficult people can be attributed to lack of process or sloppy meetings that do not address issues and that convey a sense of wasted time to participants. Developing fair, balanced procedures that generate accomplishment and create norms that can be enforced by the group is an important preventive measure.

### Working with Staff, Leaders, and Organizers

Community decision-making groups often have a community leader or organizer to assist the group with its activities. The leader or organizer receives direction from the chairperson. The chairperson also works out roles of staff members. Once roles have been established, the chairperson should avoid changing them, to ensure continuity. The chairperson must find time to work out a set of meeting strategies and tactics with staff and the leader or organizer. Once the meeting strategies have been worked out and an agenda crafted, it is the chairperson's responsibility to follow the strategies and agenda, unless something unexpected comes up. (If unanticipated events occur frequently, premeeting planning is probably inadequate.)

### Making Key Contributions in Meetings

The following four types of contributions are especially important, and the chairperson chooses areas in which to contribute, depending on what the group needs.

*Intellectual Contributions.* The chairperson makes intellectual contributions including suggesting ideas, modifying others' ideas, and blending the ideas of people in the group into a single, coherent idea. This role is assumed only if needed, not just because the chairperson is good at it. If plenty of good ideas are being suggested, the chairperson should wait until his or her input is needed.

*Interpersonal Contributions.* The chairperson may praise people who have made good contributions, see that everyone has a chance to contribute (enhancing the underparticipator), and cool down someone who is participating too much (tempering the overparticipant). Doing interpersonal work means doing all those big and little things that help the process move smoothly. Again, the chairperson should do them only when and if needed.

*Task Contributions.* Every community group and its subgroups have essential tasks to complete. Time lines provide structure to achieve the group's goals. The chairperson supports the setting of tasks and construction of time lines to complete tasks.

*Process Contributions.* Keeping everyone involved in the community process is crucial. The chairperson should be sensitive to the pace of community process, that is, the way a community does its business. Tasks must be accomplished, but participation is vital as well. Decisions need community support. Chairpeople should establish a tone and a pace that are comfortable for the community as a whole.

## LEADERSHIP RESPONSIBILITIES

An individual can be appointed to a management position but not really to a leadership role. One actually *assumes* a leadership role. Leadership involves taking new steps and thinking about new ideas and approaches. Effective leadership involves convincing others that they can comfortably follow the leader. Experienced leaders understand that leadership involves risk taking, voicing difficult problems, and setting strategic missions.

Leadership creates followership, a relationship that can be called the leadership exchange. *Leadership exchange* occurs when the leader risks himself or herself to establish future directions for the group. The new directions address knotty problems in ways that the group recognizes have potential to solve those problems and help the community, and the group rewards the leader with cooperation.

A leader does not solely advance his or her own agenda. Creating leadership exchange involves creation of new possibilities and new invitations for others to contribute. Leadership requires innovation and selflessness and, ultimately, helps a group make changes in its community.

There are two aspects to leadership—the first is outlining a possible future and the second is helping to create the conditions and excitement that encourage people to contribute to that future. Because group members are the people who make decisions, it is crucial that members contribute ideas and support. Effective leaders develop an overall vision from parts of ideas contributed by themselves and others, thus making solutions a group process.

The chairperson must distribute the role of leadership among the members of the steering groups and into the community. The empowerment principle, a conviction that holds that membership in the committee process expands a member's ability to be a leader and take a leadership role, is at work here.

Leadership is about change. A leader has to be able to change, help others change, "create change without [causing] crisis," and avoid creating too much crisis while carrying out the previous three items (personal communication with R. Quinn, professor of Management and Organizations, University of Michigan, Ann Arbor, October 11, 2011).

### Building Capacity in Others

Helping others is a key element of leadership. Leadership has a fluid quality, and leadership should pass from person to person—from chairperson to group member—as the decision-making process progresses. Chairpeople should encourage others to take leadership roles. Groups in which everyone has a role but everyone also helps everyone else are good metaphors for the meeting process. In effective groups, each member assumes some leadership, and multiple leaders are a dynamic aspect of leadership. Leadership is like a jazz orchestra: Everyone has a chance—should have a chance—to be featured, and supported by others while being featured.

### Inspiring Followership

Followership is essential to helping others lead. The best workplaces, meetings, and families are those in which all members and participants have a chance to both lead and follow. If one individual is always leading, others must always follow, and thus a routine emerges. Followership involves letting someone else move into the leadership role, both structurally ("At the upcoming meeting will you 'take the lead' on discussing this issue?") and procedurally ("I know that you have a lot of knowledge about this area. Could you get us going?").

Because it is difficult to exercise leadership in every area and on every issue, leaders need the support of followers, and few things are more discouraging to a potential leader than finding that there are no followers. Effective leadership is balanced and enhanced by effective followership.

## CONCLUSION

The chairperson is like an orchestra conductor. Chairpeople are vital to the process of community decision making. But, like the conductor, they often get work done through others. The chairperson has a challenge that can be met more easily if good working relations are established with staff and leaders or organizers, if contributions by others are encouraged, and if leadership is balanced by effective followership.

# Chapter 7
## The Community Group Member

Group members often believe that there is nothing to learn about being a member. Members may show up and doze off until the meeting is over—an attitude that is, regrettably, all too prevalent. However, members have responsibilities, and their active participation is critical to the success of the community group.

## MEMBER RESPONSIBILITIES

Group members have many responsibilities; however, most have not received instruction in fulfilling them. What follows are some of these responsibilities.

### Being Prepared

Members have a responsibility to review and think about meeting material in advance. Organizers work hard to prepare advance material for meetings, and members who come unprepared are not making an appropriate effort.

### Aiding the Chairperson

Most members believe it is the chairperson's responsibility to keep order in the meeting. If a member acts inappropriately, other members may complain later that the chairperson did not exercise proper authority or discipline. Keeping order, however, is everyone's responsibility. The chairperson cannot exercise discipline all the time. If all responsibility is ceded to the chairperson, a student–teacher relationship emerges, with the chairperson-teacher being the custodian of order, and the members-students taking no responsibility for discipline.

Group members should come to the aid of the chairperson. Members do not have to wait for the chairperson to exert control before helping out. If one member has spent several minutes attacking another member's proposal, another member might say, "I think you're being a little hard on this proposal, and you're making people feel bad about it. It has some problems; I see one or two myself, but I think we owe it to everyone to have a balanced discussion." This holds the attacking individual in check, but the chairperson did not have to exercise disciplinary measures because a member of the group did. Group members do not perform that duty often, but it is effective when they do. The chairperson will appreciate some help.

Alternately, the chairperson may make such a disciplinary comment. At that point, the chairperson would appreciate a member saying, "Yes, I agree with the chair, and perhaps we could focus on some of the positives as well as the negatives."

## Modulating Participation

Some meetings have high levels of participation, in which everyone contributes; other meetings have less participation. Members should balance their typical behavior in meetings. For example, enthusiastic members should try to hold back in meetings in which the culture and style are more subdued. It is wise to adjust one's self-presentation, because observers notice how much someone participates and adjust their view of his or her credibility as a result. The overparticipator is recognized as someone who does not give others a chance. Even though his or her ideas may be good, a member who overparticipates against group-established norms risks lowering his or her effectiveness.

A member who does not participate at all may be thought of as being critical and hostile, even if this is not true. Although it may be appropriate not to say anything, other members may think the silent member is quietly criticizing them. When members who are speaking do not know what other people are thinking, they tend to assume that the silent member is thinking about them disapprovingly. Some individuals may imagine that the silent member dislikes them. Thus, other members act toward the silent member as if he or she is hostile. This reaction is frequently a surprise to the silent member. The best course for a member who does not want to participate in a meeting is to make a comment to that effect.

### Not Dumping Problems on the Group

Many members feel that if they do not like a proposal it is enough to say, "I don't like that." However, stating the negative is insufficient; something more assertive is needed. "Dumping problems on the group" refers to the practice of expressing one's feelings and then expecting the group to find the answer to the question, "If John doesn't like this mileage proposal, what would he like?"

This question, "What would he like?" suggests an appropriate course of action. A group member should, when pointing out problems with a proposal, also suggest a solution. For example, "I really don't like this mileage proposal, because I feel there is not enough money to make it worthwhile for me to use my own car. Forty cents per mile is well below what others provide, and well below current government guidelines. However—and this may not be possible—at forty-seven cents a mile I would find myself in support." This contribution focuses the discussion on an alternative proposal rather than leaving the group to guess at what the disapproving member might prefer. In the example, the speaker recognized that the proposed higher amount might not be feasible; however, the proposal provided a focus for the discussion to move toward a goal.

### Providing Support for Other Members

Group membership requires attention to the other supporting members and their interests and needs. Members have an obligation to provide support for other members, for example, reining in one who responded too harshly to another member's proposal. Positive comments of support and appreciation are always welcome but infrequently offered. Members should listen to and validate the ideas of others, especially when new ideas are discussed. New ideas are risky, although they are needed and, in most cases, wanted. They may feel threatening, because new ideas usually mean doing things differently, and they may seem vulnerable, because they usually are incomplete. Often these two features—threat and vulnerability—create a frenzy in community groups, during which everybody jumps on the bandwagon against the new idea.

## CONCLUSION

Being a member of a community group carries responsibilities. Members need to be prepared, proactive, supportive, and engaging. Group members should think of themselves as part of a community team and realize that the team's performance determines its success.

# Chapter 8
## The Community Leader or Organizer

As mentioned earlier, community decision-making groups often have a leader or organizer who helps them do their work. The community leader or organizer frequently assumes many linked roles. Generally, he or she works on behalf of the action-planning organization to facilitate its activities and to provide information and service to decision-making groups. Because most groups do not meet all the time, someone must prepare correspondence, keep files, and do research. When the group is not in session, a leader or organizer pulls together information about relevant issues, obtains comparative information, and makes sure that all information is properly assembled.

The process of community leadership and organization is sometimes called the staffing function. *Staff* has two meanings. As a noun, it refers to employees of an organization. This use refers to line authority and reflects the hierarchy of the organization. As a verb it refers to the process of providing a specific service to a committee or board; here it implies services and comes from the "staff" part of the staff-line distinction (Simon, Thompson, & Smithburg, 1991). In the staff-line distinction, staff stand to one side and have no line, or decision-making, authority. Such authority they do have comes from knowledge, expertise, or proximity to the decision-making positions in the line organization. The community organizer or "staffer" does not have line authority, but he or she does have the authority of expertise, time, and professionalism.

Given this distinction, the most important roles a leader or organizer can assume are those of coordinator-manager, aide to chairperson, researcher and knowledge synthesizer, writer-documenter, aide to consultants, and consultant-professional expert. Although each role requires different skills and competencies, all are essential to the optimal functioning of a community group. Although this chapter is geared toward the professional leader or organizer, the information about expectations and tasks also can be helpful to volunteers.

## COORDINATOR-MANAGER

A community leader is involved in many activities as a coordinator-manager. Sometimes the problems of managing mechanics at a meeting overshadow the substantive purpose, and problems such as lack of parking, reimburse-merit concerns, and inadequate meeting rooms consume so much time that work cannot go on. The community leader's responsibility is to avoid these situations through planning and action before a meeting.

Although unique situations do arise, planning problems generally stem from lack of attention to common themes and needs. Thus, the role of the coordinator-manager is not trivial, and the mechanics of preparation are critical. Once meeting planning is under control, attention can move toward the preparation of meeting materials.

Frequently, the leader helps the chairperson prepare for meetings. In addition, in the course of his or her job, the leader learns a great deal of substantive information that he or she passes along to the chairperson or group.

## AIDE TO CHAIRPERSON

The community leader's tasks involve elements of chairperson leadership and followership. The leader is usually assigned to one or more committees or work groups, and the chairperson, within the limits of group policy and procedure, is his or her boss. Because of the work with the chair, the leader can express a number of ideas and orientations and can influence the committee. This position demonstrates the professional skill of the community leader.

Community leaders who perform well in other support roles often fail in this one because they do not develop a good working relationship with the chairperson. Mechanics (doing the work of preparation) and dynamics (establishing good interpersonal connections) are involved in establishing this good working relationship.

There often are many different aspects of and perspectives on the issue that the chair and committee are considering. Although the community leader may have his or her own perspective, it should be subordinate to those of the chairperson and the committee. While writing policy, the leader should clearly distinguish between the opinions of the group and his or her own recommendations. The community leader is a professional, often trained in a distinct field. Training, professional status, and background give the leader special responsibility for developing her or his view, but the leader is only a knowledgeable servant of the committee and the chairperson. The leader must act ethically, letting the committee and chairperson act in the capacities to which they have been appointed while helping them make appropriate decisions.

However, the community leader may express his or her views to the chairperson in private, initiating such discussions early in the process to learn the chairperson's perspective on particular topics. Such discussions continue throughout the leader–chairperson relationship and should ensure that no surprises occur regarding the leader's understanding of the chairperson's positions.

A community leader–chairperson conference should be part of the procedures of all leaders and chairpeople. A conference can take place after agenda items have been determined and the leader is preparing a preliminary agenda for the chairperson's review and approval. After this, the discussion—what is the order of agenda items, what are people likely to do at this meeting, what are other problems, and so forth—should turn to elements of meeting planning. Often, the leader and chairperson ignore this crucial conference, and the pair must improvise after the meeting begins. Regular, informal meetings between leader and chairperson are the basis for a positive working relationship.

During these meetings, the community leader briefs the chairperson on upcoming issues and concerns and shares intelligence reports. The leader should determine whether the chairperson needs additional information so that the information can be gathered in time for the meeting. Together, the leader and the chairperson consider meeting strategy and tactics and share thoughts and perspectives.

Beyond its helpful role in understanding the dynamics that may emerge during a community meeting, this informal session between leader and chairperson is crucial to meeting preparation. The leader plays a relatively neutral role during the meeting; he or she takes minutes and does not participate emotionally in the process. The chairperson, in seeking to convey a statesmanlike posture, also participates in a neutral way, tempering the hot-headed and firing up the lukewarm. Therefore, prior ventilation of feelings is proper preparation for remaining effectively neutral during the meeting.

## RESEARCHER AND KNOWLEDGE SYNTHESIZER

As a resource and knowledge synthesizer, the community leader's job is twofold. First, he or she is responsible for securing knowledge and presenting it to the committee in a form that can be used for decision-making purposes. Second, she or he must be alert to and synthesize the many interpersonal aspects of knowledge sharing.

Regarding the first task, the leader should not approach research in a scholarly or scientific mode, undertaking time-consuming, in-depth literature reviews. Procedures need to be developed for quick but thorough literature surveys and for delivering state-of-the-art briefings. The leader may want to use a meta-analysis, which scans all recent studies on a topic, to determine what the evidence points to.

The community leader or organizer is a knowledge synthesizer and communicator rather than a knowledge developer. The contributions he or she makes to knowledge come from developing fresh information—finding new categories through which information can be gathered and pulling together split or fragmented information.

This part of the job is theoretical or conceptual, but it is here that the community leader can affect the thinking of the committee. A key element in managing ideas is to have ideas, and the ability to come up with new ideas or to present old ideas with new twists that make them useful is an important skill. To do this, the leader needs to gather information from many sources.

### Staff Sources

Some information is already in the possession of the community leader, because he or she usually has expertise in some substantive area of competence, such as criminal justice, social planning, child welfare, or community organization.

### Libraries, Data Banks, and Compilations of Abstracts and Dissertations

The standard academic sources of information—library sources, data banks, and compilations of abstracts and dissertations—should be checked first. However, the community leader must go beyond this checking to develop personal resources that augment his or her ability to obtain information quickly. Leaders should get to know reference librarians. Most individuals do not know enough about libraries, and a reference librarian can find information quickly. It is sometimes appropriate to hire a librarian to do an initial search and assemble copies of relevant material for the leader to review. Much time is wasted looking for material that could be gathered more efficiently by someone more familiar with information sources.

### Search Engines

The community leader can often begin with popular Internet-based search engines such as Google. A quick scan of a search can provide a number of titles. A better-refined search will find abstracts of articles that can be printed and mailed or, if the database is on site, made immediately available to the searcher. This process shortens the search and allows the leader to spend time synthesizing, instead of collecting, information.

### Social Networking

The most interesting technological development since the first edition of this book is the explosion of social networking. Of particular relevance to community leadership and organization is the new field of community informatics. The Wikipedia ("Community informatics," 2011) discussion on this topic begins as follows:

Community informatics (CI), also known as community networking, electronic community networking, community-based technologies or community technology, refers to an emerging field of investigation and practice concerned with principles and norms related to information and communication technology (ICT) with a focus on the personal, social, cultural or economic development of, within and by communities. It is formally located as an academic discipline within a variety of academic faculties including Information Science, Information Systems, Computer Science, Planning, Development Studies, and Library Science among others and draws on insights on community development from a range of social sciences disciplines. It is a cross- or interdisciplinary approach interested in the utilization of ICTs for different forms of community action, as distinct from pure academic study or research about ICT effects.

Many journals and research projects report on this emerging field, which focuses directly on community resources, community connections, and mobilizing leading and organizing communities.

### Knowledgeable Individuals

The community leader should know key knowledgeable individuals to call to seek information on the issues under consideration; for example, lawyers are essential when legal questions arise. This technique is usually effective for locating the main points of a developing line of thought; more conventional research can provide additional answers. Networking is one kind of relationship sourcing. A leader typically has both professional and community-based individuals in his or her network with whom he or she can talk and from whom information is available.

### News Media and Professional Publications

Community leaders should read at least one national and one local newspaper daily and subscribe to professional publications. Community members expect that the leader will be knowledgeable about current events; he or she is expected to be the eyes and ears of the committee and do the reading and listening that members cannot do. The leader should be proactive in sharing information and bringing it to the attention of the committee. An item or a conference announcement should attract the attention of the leader if it relates to the work of the chairperson and committee, and he or she should bring it to the attention of the chairperson. However, the popular press should be approached cautiously as a source of technical information; in many cases when research is reported by the press, important qualifications slip away from the initial report of the story or do not catch the reporter's attention.

### Political Considerations

The community leader should remember that data have emotional as well as rational dimensions. Simple factual reports may create problems for committee members. For example, reporting on the average weight of the members of the community and discussing weight as a health risk may trouble some committee members who are struggling with weight-control problems. Issues about teenage parenting may cause a reaction from a group member whose teenager is a parent. Discussion of the broken family index may be difficult for a committee member who is divorced. Other types of considerations include the following.

### Minority Interests

The community leader should determine whether there are any special minority interests in a policy under consideration and what information would be helpful to them.

### Committee-Boss Constituency

The community leader should be aware of any implications a policy proposal has for the constituency of any members of the committee. In addition, the community leader should be informed about implications for the executive of the agency who retained him or her (if it is not the committee itself). Being able to foresee possible effects allows the affected parties to take early action.

### Uninvolved Groups

The community leader or organizer should give thought to groups or individuals who have been left out of the decision-making process because no one initially thought of asking them to participate or considered their needs. This omission is serious, because the left-out group was unable to provide input, because any solution will not be inclusive, and because the slighted group may oppose the proposed solution out of anger.

### Political-Scientific Conflicts

Such conflicts occur when science and scientific popular will clash. For example, a discussion of the importance of fathers in the family and the dangers to children in families without fathers may cause conflicts with lesbian households where an adoption or artificial insemination has occurred, or with members of a subcommunity with a large number of single-mother families.

### Personal Issues

Individuals have personal sensitivities and concerns. For example, female, Jewish, or African American group members usually dislike being asked, "Well, what do women (or Jews, or blacks) think about this issue?" The community leader needs to be culturally and personally aware of possible sensitivities.

## WRITER-DOCUMENTER

The role of the writer-documenter is an extension of the role of knowledge synthesizer, but this role stresses formal exchange of information. The knowledge that the community leader pulls together is generally given to the committee in writing, as background information for its work. The leader is usually responsible for writing most proposals that go before the committee. This aspect of the job is among the most frustrating because writing and rewriting is quite labor-intensive. In addition, the leader usually takes meeting minutes, and these minutes have special importance to the committee's work.

### KNOWER System

Community leaders can use the KNOWER system when writing drafts and documents for community groups (Tropman, 1984). The system is an acronym using the following terms:

- KNowledge
- Organization in the form of an outline that is approved by the chairperson, consultants, and other relevant individuals
- Writing the draft
- Evaluation of the initial product by others
- Rewriting the draft, often several times

Writing is one key aspect of the leader's job, and many community group members and organizers do not know what community workers think until they see it on paper. Writing also can reveal sloppy thinking and encourage revision and refinement of the thought process.

It is important for the community leader to maintain a balanced perspective when writing, because a written document provides the opportunity to introduce bias into the content. The leader or organizer should resist this temptation, because his or her influence must be given in more open ways, rather than through subtle changes in the text. If the committee believes that the leader cannot be trusted, his or her influence with the committee erodes.

The leader should rewrite draft information to avoid the process of group editing. Once a group reads a written draft, the urge to edit or rewrite is almost overwhelming. If rewriting drafts is a problem for the leader, group editing will be especially troublesome. A good technique is to ask members for comments, put these on the draft, and review and make appropriate changes to the document after the meeting. The leader can blend the various comments into improvements.

## Types of Written Documents

Technical reports, policy drafts, and meeting minutes are the three main types of written materials the community leader manages.

*Technical Reports.* Assembling scientific and technical material that the reports committee will consider is the most complicated writing the leader does. For this material to be meaningful and useful, it must be more than a recitation of what others have said; the technical report must be a synthesis of common elements, a balance of varied points of view, and an attempt to show where the weight of evidence lies. Most material the community leader uses in writing policy materials for consideration will be unfamiliar to committee members. Care must be taken to provide correct reporting and accurate reflection of the differences that exist in the material. The leader should keep copies of all materials in a file. When the syntheses are prepared, the leader should make a list of references or footnotes to specific sources and quotes so they may be checked later for accuracy and the reference material will be available when decisions are made.

*Policy Drafts.* Committee members have a strong interest in policy drafts, usually reading every word. For the draft, the leader should begin with the main issue and, while still on the first page, add proposed or revised text during the meeting. If the text is long, the leader can request copies be returned with notations, harmonizing the various suggestions later.

The leader should be aware of his or her psychological reaction to the review that follows. His or her feelings may be hurt if the committee ignores reports; however, too much attention is likely to generate the feeling of nit-picking. Overattention, however, is preferable to underattention in this case.

Because the policy document represents the committee to the public, members examine it in detail. However, even the most experienced leader cannot anticipate all the nuances of words and the implications these may have for people from different backgrounds and areas of expertise. Therefore, the leader should prepare, both psychologically and procedurally, for a careful review. (One system for review is suggested in the section on "Decision Rules" in chapter 12). Such review means many revisions; five or six are not atypical. If the leader is aware that this process will take place, he or she can prepare to work within it.

*Meeting Minutes.* Meeting minutes are often a source of difficulty. Although there is no standard form for writing minutes, some guidelines do exist. *Process minutes,* in which the community leader tries to record the process of the meeting like a tape recorder, is an ineffective method for taking minutes. The central purpose and content of the meeting can become buried under a wave of process. *Content minutes* is a solution to this problem. In this style of minutes-taking, the headings, attendance record, date, and other points remain the same; however, after that the minutes follow a specific form. (See Appendix C for sample minutes.)

- *Agenda connect.* Along the side of the paper are headings that correspond to agenda topics. Thus, the reader can easily follow the agenda right into the minutes.
- *Summative reflection.* Content minutes aim to capture the main points of a discussion for the reader; no names are used.
- *Decision.* The main decision is recorded and bolded. Some may even highlight the decision in a special font; record names, dates, and assignments; and box the decision so that it is easily identifiable.

Well-prepared minutes provide a model of focused discussion; they highlight decisions and provide a means to check and determine what needs to be done, by whom, and when. The essence of arguments made in the meeting is recorded. Some skill is necessary for judging, evaluating, and fairly reporting different points of view. For this reason, the community leader is the most appropriate individual to take minutes. If there is no leader, minutes can be taken by group members on a rotating basis.

The message that the minutes give to the members is more important than the simple record-keeping function. Groups waste valuable meeting time reviewing old minutes and correcting them; this time can be saved if the leader takes precise, economical minutes that do not invite endless recapitulation.

Minutes provide a record of who participated in the decision making. For this reason, a list of those present and absent is important. The list provides information about who was involved in a particular decision, information that often is crucial later. Names are listed in alphabetical order. The chairperson's title follows her or his name in parentheses. This convention is far more important than might be suspected. Members can read departure from alphabetical order as an order of status, even if such a message is not intended. It can be devastating to those who find their names at the bottom of the list. The community leader lists himself or herself on a separate line, emphasizing the distinction between the leader and the community group members.

It is almost impossible to take good minutes while participating fully in a meeting; for this reason the community leader should temper his or her participation in meetings. The role of the leader should be that of participant-observer; a minutes-taker must observe and listen carefully to what is going on. The process is important both for accurately recording minutes and for understanding committee dynamics.

While participating in the meeting, the community leader responds to questions and provides clarifications to material for which he or she is responsible. The role of minute taker can be used to help clarify discussion through the guise of clarifying the minutes. If the leader thinks that a decision is not clear, he or she can ask permission to read back what he or she understands the decision to be. The group members can provide clarification.

## AIDE TO CONSULTANTS

Community decision-making groups sometimes have the assistance of consultants, both for substantive issues like economic development and process or technical issues like conflict management. These individuals could be from a nearby university or local talent bank.

Involving consultants requires skill and balance. If the consultants remain too far from the process, they are unhelpful. If they are too close, they become overinvolved and may dominate the process. The community leader has an important responsibility in managing or orchestrating consultants, both in person and by providing them information.

The community leader needs to know the consultants and their capabilities. He or she should seek, with the help of the chairperson, to create a flow of information and assistance to and from the consultants. Sometimes consultants assist the leader directly, discussing ideas and reviewing drafts and other written materials. Consultants also can attend meetings to provide technical support and prepare written documents. All consultant activities should be organized through the leader.

## CONSULTANT AND PROFESSIONAL EXPERT

The community leader has professional expertise and is expected to share it. Therefore, he or she sometimes acts as the consultant. Such sharing must be done within the context of the knowledgeable servant, so that decision making remains at the community level. Key skills to act as a consultant include the following:

- listening actively
- responding empathetically and sympathetically
- giving corrective and supportive feedback
- challenging ideas tactfully but forcefully
- crafting problem-solving rather than fault-finding conversation
- suggesting stimulating, innovative approaches.

## WORKING THE MEETING

Regardless of preparation, much of what happens in community decision-making groups occurs in meetings. Experience and good judgment about participation are crucial. The seen-but-not-heard rule is good to follow for the beginning community leader, because it is better to err by being too quiet than by overparticipating. It is much easier to increase participation than to trim the level of participation once a pattern of meeting involvement has been established.

In the community meeting, the leader can play a role of modest, technical participation, always being careful not to undermine the chairperson. The leader can elaborate on reports, offer factual comments, and seek clarification of the comments of others with regard to facts. He or she can offer to obtain additional information on sensitive points. Such an offer made in a strategic, timely fashion could serve to diffuse a potentially inflammatory situation.

The community leader plays the role of supportive expert. Sometimes in meetings the leader or organizer must support ideas that have been developed, add technical validation where important, and head off potential conflicts. When problematic issues arise—for example, a member states something that is technically incorrect—it is best to approach that person at a break. Only under extreme circumstances, for example, if the technical error becomes the basis for action, should the leader correct someone publicly.

## WORKING BEHIND THE SCENES

In addition to meeting participation, much of what the community leader does is behind the scenes, although not under the table. The leader has both task and process goals, among them helping the community achieve action aims and helping the community become more cohesive. The leader sometimes works both sides of the street to provide this help. On one hand, he or she encourages task completion; on the other hand, he or she supports appropriate process. Usually the leader does whatever is not being done. Thus, if the community group members are too task-focused, the leader reminds them of process; if too much process is going on, the leader stresses task goals.

However, problems can arise in this process if the leader does not know the community well. Egan (1994) discussed potential "minefields"; although he focused primarily on organizations, his points apply to communities as well.

### Covert Culture

Communities have values, beliefs, and attitudes that affect the way members see the world, think about things, and explain events. The leader must learn about this culture by getting to know the community.

### Social System

Communities have patterns of behavior as well as patterns of culture. Such behavior often represents a combination of public and hidden ways that things are done. The leader needs to know the community's locally based patterns.

### Idiosyncratic Individuals

People can be difficult (Bramson, 1981), or powerful, or just unique. The leader needs to spend time in the community so that he or she can get a flavor of who is influential. Once opinion leaders have been identified, the leader should spend personal time with them, if possible.

### Community Politics

Politics is about who does what for whom—about gains and losses, money, power, prestige, and access to jobs. Politics are always present in a community. The leader needs to know the lay of the political land and be prepared to encounter selfishness, self-centeredness, and greed. He or she should remain focused on helping partisans to become community citizens, preparing himself or herself for loss while working for gain.

## CONCLUSION

The professional community leader has many important tasks, and each has unique features. The leader's success will be enhanced if she or he learns how to do each of these jobs well. Greater group success can be achieved if the members also are aware of these jobs. Sometimes the leader has to educate volunteers about the range and limitations of his or her particular tasks; therefore, the leader must be thoroughly knowledgeable about the dimensions of his or her positions and roles.

# Part Three
## Conducting Effective Community Group Meetings

Associations of community members do their work in community meetings, and every day numerous meetings address America's social concerns. People discuss and decide what they would like to see in the future of their communities. Often, these meetings do not go well. In one of our country's great paradoxes, our emphasis on associations has not been matched with a broadly accepted, constantly improving, technology for effective group work. The meeting, which is the central mechanism for decision and discussion, is among the most poorly guided of social institutions. It is almost as if there is a bizarre inversion: The more we depend on meetings, the less we know about how to manage them well.

The supposed ineptitude of boards and committees is expressed in dozens of humorous asides, such as "a camel is a horse assembled by a committee," "a board is a group that takes minutes to waste hours," or "a board member is synonymous with dead wood."

Partly because of our individualistic society, group efforts are hard to manage in the United States. People frequently use comments such as, "I didn't get any work done; I had to spend the entire day in meetings." This phrase tells a lot about the assumptions of where work is done (alone in our offices) and the extent to which group activities (meetings) interfere with, rather than become central to, work.

No matter how good one's intentions, community development success will remain elusive unless individuals in the community meet, process information, and come up with decisions. What should such a process look like, and what do we know about how to manage it?

Participant-observation research on "meeting masters" conducted at the University of Michigan provides some guidance (Tropman, 2006). Meeting masters are women and men who have the reputation for running excellent meetings. Many of these individuals worked with community and citizens' committees. Others hailed from government, human services organizations, and corporations. In this context, an excellent meeting was defined as having three elements:

Decisions get made.

The decisions are of high quality.

Participants enjoy themselves.

Almost anyone can produce meetings and committees and meet these three criteria for success. But it requires planning—plan the work; work the plan! Making the most of the opportunity for group leadership involves doing good work in meetings. This section provides community workers with the terminology and techniques to make this happen. Chapter 9 focuses on the perspectives meeting masters had about community meetings. Chapter 10 attends to the process of community meetings. Chapter 11 deals with the skills of guiding community group discussion. Chapter 12 provides help in moving community groups to decisions. Chapter 13 provides some suggestions in structuring assessment: Has the group achieved anything and, if so, is it any good?

# Chapter 9
## The Effective Meeting: Managing Perspectives

One of the most striking things about meeting masters is their perspective on community meetings. Meeting masters think about their meetings in ways different from accepted convention. Although most group members, community leaders, and community organizers view community meetings with a sense of hopelessness, meeting masters view them as a mechanism to enact the community's vision.

## PRINCIPLES OF MEETING MASTERS

The philosophy of meeting masters is summarized in the following seven principles. None is complicated or strange. However, the negative culture of community meetings is so deeply entrenched that we complain, but we cannot stop to make improvements. Note that each principle has a caution section that mentions stumbling blocks that may make these seemingly easy ideas harder to implement.

### Conceptual Principle

Meeting masters did not talk about having meetings. They talked about producing meetings, as in a drama, or giving a meeting, as in a party. This perspective brings in a planning mindset.

> *Caution:* Not everyone will find this perspective comfortable initially.

### Purpose Principle

Have a purpose. Each meeting or series of meetings that meeting masters are involved with has a purpose stated in writing. The statement of purpose, similar to a vision or mission statement, focuses the group's activities. In addition, the statement brings important differences in perspectives among individuals to the surface early in the process and allows prompt resolution of these.

> *Caution:* Some group members do not want to take the time to clarify purposes. These individuals should be consulted before the meeting begins.

### Orchestra Principle

Meeting masters regard their meetings as if they are an orchestra or theater performance. There is a score or script (agenda, minutes, and reports) and rehearsal (members working on the material in their minds or holding conversations before the meeting begins, using their "scripts"). If necessary, there are costumes (the ambience created by the meeting dress code and related to roles). The meeting is seen as the culmination of a preparatory process, not the beginning. One meeting master compared the preparation she did for a meeting to that done for a dinner party at her home.

She organizes the tasks so that when the guests arrive everything is ready—the food has been selected, and cooking has begun. She did not tell people as they entered the house, "I wasn't sure what you wanted to eat, so I didn't start anything. I thought I could work that out once you got here." Instead, no effort is spared to create a welcoming, hospitable climate, allowing guests to focus on interaction. The same principle is at work in the orchestra principle. Preparation, organization, and thought can create an outstanding performance.

> *Caution:* Some group members claim they do not have the time to prepare for meetings. Actually, they do, but they have other priorities. Remind these members of the four-to-one ratio: Four hours are saved for every one hour spent in planning a meeting.

### Three-Characters Principle

Meeting masters believe there are only three things one does at a community meeting—make announcements, make decisions, and brainstorm items for future meetings. Meeting masters organize their agendas in that way; meetings are driven by the content or character of agenda items rather than by the people present. Meetings begin with announcements and then proceed to the items for decision. Advance work has identified the items on which the group needs to act, and appropriate preparatory work has been done. After decisions are made, meeting masters shift to the brainstorming items.

> *Caution:* This principle requires that group members think about the nature of the items they want to discuss, something most never do.

### No-More-Reports Principle

Many meetings are not meetings at all; they are oral reports or newsletters in which individuals tell what they or their subgroup has been doing. There is no need for this, and meeting masters instead focus on issues. Meeting masters contact individuals in advance who might want to deliver a report (for example, from a finance or planning committee). The meeting master helps to organize the content along three character lines. If the content is an announcement, it is given during the announcement section of the agenda. If the content is an item for action or decision, it is put in that section of the agenda. If the item is for discussion and feedback but no decision needs to be made, it is put in the brainstorming section of the agenda. In this way all of the same content is covered but in a more economical and efficient way, with a focus on and identification of exactly what was hoped for when a particular item was introduced. Significant time is saved.

This process differs markedly from the meeting at which a chairperson invites everyone to give a report. In this meeting style, the agenda is driven by those who give reports. These members may have some announcements, some items for decisions, and some items for discussion. Because little thought has been given and little advance organization prepared, even the person who gives the report is sometimes confused about whether an item is up for decision, discussion, or announcement. In the no-more-reports meeting style, every item is already on the agenda and has its place.

> *Caution:* People like to talk. Group members may be attached to their reports and not understand that giving them violates the three-characters principle and can waste time. Meeting masters should work with members to promote the advantages of this new style.

### No-New-Business Principle

Meeting masters believe that new business is distracting. Typically, new business is ill formulated and requires an inordinate amount of time to explore its nature. It can be an invitation for those who are not prepared for the meeting to delay the meeting by focusing on the new business. Meeting masters invite group members to send items for the agenda in advance. This approach puts people in a more thoughtful, more reflective mode when they are suggesting items for discussion and action.

> *Caution:* The old style of "show up and spew out" at meetings is deeply ingrained in our culture. To avoid appearing heavy handed, meeting masters can ask group members who want to discuss new topics to wait until the end of the meeting and use what time is left for discussion.

### Role Principle

When things go wrong in meetings, group members are inclined to blame individuals who, they feel, have acted inappropriately. Members may feel that if they could only get rid of those meddlesome, troublesome people, the group process would go well. However, the role of the troublesome person is set up in the context of the dynamics of the group, and if that person should leave, somebody else would step into the role. Problem behaviors can be viewed as roles in the community play. The best way to change roles is to change the script, not the actor. Rescripting the meeting with a carefully prepared agenda and reports will help deal with problems previously thought of as personality differences.

> *Caution:* Finding fault with people is common. Meeting masters have to listen to a lot of off-the-record blaming as the transition to better community meetings takes place.

### High-Quality-Decisions Principle

Meeting masters espouse a deep conviction that meetings are information-processing systems, the output of which are decisions. They do not view meetings as social gatherings or places to chat and meet people, although those things happen. Using the orchestra principle, meeting masters take the view that they get together in meetings to do work, and the work they do is to review information from a variety of sources and make decisions. These decisions must be of high quality. Meetings are not a matter of coming together, quickly making a decision, and adjourning for a cup of coffee; rather, they are deliberate and serious. To emphasize this point, meeting masters sponsor a process of auditing meetings and decisions. For example, groups can look back after a time and examine the decisions they have made. Members can ask, "Here's what we've done during the past six months. Is it any good?" For well-run meetings, the answer will be yes. This commitment to high quality in the decision-making process creates among group members the sense that they are doing something important. Looking at the importance of a group fundamentally changes the character of the meetings from a group of people who get together "to take minutes and waste hours" to a group of people who get together to make a difference in their community.

> *Caution:* The idea that a committee ought to actually do something is radical enough; insistence that that something be of high quality is an added shocker. However, making high-quality decisions may appeal to committee members, because this concept can be used to drive other committee procedures. People are encouraged to say, "If we want to do something for our community that is worthwhile, here is what we have to do and the ways we have to organize for this to happen."

## CONCLUSION

Managing perspectives is crucial to becoming a meeting master. In meetings run by meeting masters, there is a sense that expectations are different. Before these meetings even begin, they have an aura of success. In productive meetings, there is a sense of achievement and accomplishment, and this can be reproduced in any group.

# Chapter 10
## The Effective Meeting: Managing Process

Meeting masters approach community group meetings by addressing four items:

- *Planning*. Meeting masters organize meetings, decide what topics should be on the agenda, and ensure group members have access to the agenda and other information before the meeting.
- *Preparation*. Meeting masters manage preparation. Meeting planning differs from meeting preparation in the same way that meal planning differs from meal preparation. Meal planning focuses on what the menu should be, the components, and people's choices for food. Meal preparation focuses on getting the meal ready just before it is time to eat. Meeting preparation focuses on the order of the agenda and ordering items needed for the meeting.
- *Paper*. Meeting masters are sensitive to the volume of paper that group members receive and try to make the amount reasonable, intelligible, and accurate.
- *Integrity*. Meeting masters manage process integrity by honoring time commitments and agenda.

MANAGING PLANNING

In planning meetings, meeting masters follow three rules: the rule of halves, the rule of sixths, and the rule of three-fourths.

## Rule of Halves

Following the rule of halves, community group members can and should give proposed agenda topics and information to the chairperson or community leader any time from the end of the last meeting until halfway before the next meeting. Then the chairperson, leader, or both, organize the topics.

For example, a community group that meets every month decides to use the rule of halves. At the end of the January 31 meeting, the chairperson announces that from that time until the middle of February, individuals should consider the items they would like on the agenda for the February meeting; they are invited to send those items to the chairperson. At that point in the meeting, someone might suggest that other topics be discussed. The chairperson, with the assistance of the leader, keeps a list of those items and others that are proposed after the meeting until the halfway point. At that point, the chairperson and leader meet to sift and sort the topics.

The process of sifting involves determining which of the submitted items are meeting related. Items are submitted sometimes by people who have personal reasons for suggesting them, and these cannot be handled effectively during the meeting. Those items are set aside and dealt with in an appropriate way, and the individuals who suggested them are informed about the decision. The members get feedback about what happened to their suggestions, and the items do not clutter a full meeting agenda.

The process of sorting identifies the character of each agenda item—is it an item for announcement, decision, or brainstorming? Sorting may require contacting the member who made the suggestion and obtaining clarification. Sometimes this involves discussing what will happen to the item he or she suggested. This process of crystallizing items helps focus the agenda.

Thought has been given to what will happen to each item submission. The designations of amendments, decisions, or discussion items are not inflexible. However, when proper thought has been given, they allow the chairperson and the leader to easily establish the agenda.

## Rule of Sixths

After agenda items are organized following the rule of halves, they should be tested by the rule of sixths. Approximately one-sixth of the agenda items should be from past discussions; these items still need closure. If past items comprise more than one-sixth of the agenda, it is likely that the community group is experiencing decision-avoidance psychosis, and this problem should be addressed. About four-sixths of the agenda items are current, here-and-now items. About one-sixth of the agenda items are future-oriented. They could, for example, be economic development scenarios or developments in the state that could affect the local community.

Group members should have substantial input in these future agenda items. Because most groups get items too late in the decision cycle (like coming into a restaurant late in the evening), members' ability to influence the item is often limited (you must eat what the chef has left). However, if items are brought to group members well in advance of their need for closure, the group has decision-making input. Nothing excites members more than the opportunity to see their suggestions, ideas, and perspectives incorporated into the decision-making process. This creates energy and drive, makes the committee an exciting place to be, and upgrades the quality of participation.

### Rule of Three-Fourths

The rule of three-fourths is the mail rule, and it requires planning and thinking ahead. Meeting masters do not hand out material at meetings, but they send it ahead of time so that group members can think about the information and come prepared for discussion. The leader, having finalized the agenda in consultation with the chairperson, mails the agenda, minutes, and any reports or executive summaries after about three-fourths of the interval between meetings has passed. For a monthly meeting, three weeks is close enough to the next meeting so that people will read the material, yet not so far ahead of the next meeting that people will set it aside.

## MANAGING PREPARATION

With the structure for planning in place and the planning underway, meeting masters spend time in preparation and use the rule of two-thirds and the rule of the agenda bell.

### Rule of Two-Thirds

The rule of two-thirds divides the meeting into three parts: getting started at the beginning, heavy work flow in the middle, and decompression at the end. The decompression begins at approximately the two-thirds point. Hence, during a morning meeting that lasts from 9 a.m. until noon, participants begin to lose interest around 11 a.m. Meeting masters consider this possible loss of interest when they plan the agenda.

Meeting masters use the three-characters principle to structure the agenda. The first third of the meeting begins with minutes. The minutes are quickly reviewed, any changes noted, and the group moves on. If there is not a quorum, meeting masters approve the minutes with those who are present and reintroduce them later. Minutes are followed by announcements, short items of interest and straightforward statements of unexciting facts. Exciting facts—things group members will want to discuss and think about—are saved for the discussion and brainstorming section. Meeting masters then divide the decision items into three parts: easy items, moderately difficult items, and the most difficult items. These items are arranged in a way as described in Figure 10-1.

Agenda Bell Rule

Figure 10-1, the Agenda Bell, shows how meeting masters organize items according to the agenda bell. For example, the minutes are followed by announcements. Then the items are divided, with the easy items first and more difficult items second, each one more difficult than the previous item. The most difficult item for the meeting is last, and it is placed between about the 33 percent point and the 66 percent point (or the two-thirds point). After the toughest item is dealt with, the group shifts to discussion and brainstorming items.

Meeting masters use the agenda bell to move issues forward. The meeting can start on time if it begins with minutes; latecomers have missed little. In addition, people who need to leave early probably will not leave before the two-thirds point. As a result, most group members will be present for all decision items.

The middle of the meeting, when attendance is greatest and psychological and physiological energy is highest, is when the group is working on its decision-making tasks. Meeting masters use group energy, an often-squandered resource, to help with their tasks. Meeting masters invoke a strategy of success through small wins. By putting the easy items first, the likelihood of success is higher. The pleasure of success and the desire to

FIGURE 10-1: The Agenda Bell

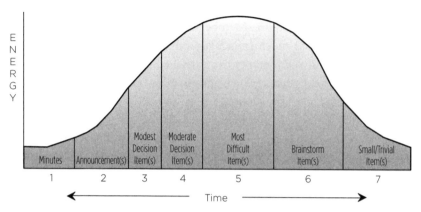

leverage success to accomplish more are the underlying dynamics of the ordering of items. This structure is self-reinforcing. Once group members experience the pleasure of accomplishment, they seek it again.

Discussion, which is less intense than decision, can most appropriately take place in the decompression phase when group members are less energized. Discussion has its own re-energizing elements, because the group is exploring exciting topics for the future.

## MANAGING PAPER

Meeting masters focus on the paper that individuals receive. In an attempt to inform members, many community groups overinform them with an avalanche of documentation. Often, group members set aside these fat packets of information. The problem is that more material means less information. The reverse—less means more—is also true. Meeting masters use the executive-summary technique to lighten the packet and embrace the contradiction.

### Executive-Summary Technique

All reports given to community group members should have an executive summary. When meeting materials are mailed, the executive summary, not the full report, is sent; group members can subsequently request the full report. Thus, a typical premeeting information packet consists of the agenda, minutes, and executive summaries (possibly four to six) that agenda topics might require. Members will read such a packet; although they do not have as much information as a full report, they have key information. Many community groups schedule a half-hour to an hour reading time before the meeting begins to allow members to examine the full documentation of the reports.

### The Agenda

Generally phrased items (old business, new business) should be avoided in constructing the agenda. More detailed text—like the "dishes" on a restaurant menu—is informative and useful to participants. A brief explanation beneath the item will help group members, just as small explanations below the dish on restaurant menus assist diners. For example, an agenda item such as "Van purchase agreement" is a good start; a sentence underneath that reads: "Finance committee recommends the purchase of six vans at $12,000 each," gives group members more information. (See Appendix A for a sample agenda.)

To the right on the agenda, one of three key words from the three-characters principle—announcement, decision/action, or brainstorming—should be listed. This reminder helps people think about the context in which an item is being offered. The context is different if an item requires a decision rather than just discussion; closure is hoped for in the first instance and openness and freedom in the second.

On the right side of the agenda, consider putting times. As one meeting master said, "An agenda without a clock is like a menu without prices. It gives you that 'uncertain feeling' that you might have committed yourself to something that you can't really handle." The times on the agenda provide suggested frameworks for the items and show how all the items can be handled (more or less) if the group sticks to suggested times.

### Rule of Minutes

Meeting masters give special attention and time to meeting minutes, using a system called content minutes. Content minutes facilitate the decision-making process, reinforce the process for the group, keep a record of what happened at the meeting, and encourage completion of tasks agreed on at the meeting. Content minutes, rather than process minutes, use a summative reflection paragraph to explain what happened rather than a narrative of the "he said, she said" variety.

The minute-taker listens to the discussion and takes notes. However, rather than using specific phrases (except for illustrative purposes), the minute taker prepares a summary of the discussion in which the points are presented logically rather than in the order they were spoken during the meeting. Discussion, whether it involves decision or discussion issues, rightfully tends to be unruly and chaotic; an idea strikes someone and he or she shares it. In turn, this creates an issue for others, who mention their ideas, and so on. Trying to record everything that everyone said is not a sensible way to record the deeper sense of the meeting. (See Appendix C for a sample of meeting minutes and chapter 8, "Writer-Documenter" section, for additional discussion of minutes.)

Meeting masters ensure that individuals who have been assigned a task for the next or a subsequent meeting receive a copy of the minutes early, even if the minutes have not been officially approved. In this way, minutes serve as a reminder memo.

## MANAGING INTEGRITY

Meeting masters are careful to ensure that time commitments are kept both for and between meetings. In addition, meeting masters pay attention to agenda integrity and spend time working out the agenda. It would be inappropriate to change the agenda after group members have received it; members will not prepare for a meeting if they know they will not have a chance to discuss the material they have prepared.

## CONCLUSION

Managing the process means paying attention to the details that can derail a meeting. Planning and organizing the agenda are crucial. Sending out the right amount of paper—enough to be helpful but not so much as to be off-putting—is also important. Respecting the work put into the agenda and preparing for it is vital as well. These techniques are not hard to use, and they pay huge dividends.

# Chapter 11
## The Effective Meeting: Managing Discussion

Group discussions often produce no results; although there is much talking, no real progress occurs in the decision-making process. Managing discussion to ensure high-quality decisions is an essential part of the successful community process. There are many ways to organize discussion at meetings. To be effective, discussions must have several elements.

- *Discussions must be based on information.* In most areas of community interest, ample information is available. Some of the information is technical, and consultants and other professionals can help interpret it. Although opinions are important, they should not be a substitute for the facts needed to make high-quality decisions.
- *Decision/action discussions should be systematic and build toward a decision.* The chairperson, the leader, and group members should periodically stop the discussion, check the progress of the group, and organize the next steps.
- *Brainstorming discussions should aim toward alternative generation and then, alternative reduction.* Brainstorming discussions should be broadly participative, nonjudgmental, and aimed toward developing a range of options and determining whether there is some underlying structure or grouping to the options.
- *More productive discussions have a problem-solving or problem-managing nature.* In problem solving and problem managing, there

is a goal to achieve, a decision to make, or a difficult issue to resolve. The problem-solving orientation provides a focus for the discussion. Contributions should be encouraged as long as they contribute to progress in problem-solving. If needed, a participant can be asked how his or her comment relates to the problem. If people bring up problems, ask them what they suggest for a solution.

## AVOIDING COMMUNICATION BARRIERS

Organizing the discussion is a key step in managing discussion. Simply pointing people in the right direction does not always work, however, because barriers interfere with the decision process and make the exchange of information difficult. The following are some of the most common barriers in community groups.

### An Overdeveloped Sense of Responsibility

Some people feel that it is solely their responsibility to speak for certain issues or certain groups. Effective group discussion allows all members to speak on all issues. Some individuals might have more knowledge than others, but all thoughtful comments are welcome.

### Poor Listening

Members of a community group often do not listen. Active listening involves attentive behavior with some or all of the following signals:

- eye contact with the speaker
- nods of comprehension as points are explained
- occasional factual and nonhostile questions
- rephrasing and sharing with the speaker to ensure all listeners understand.

Active listening does not occur when people are edgily waiting to get into the conversation, when body language clearly shows disgust with the ideas being presented, or when hostile terms are used. Active listening should be promoted by modeling good listening behavior (Bolton, 1986). Phrases such as "Let's listen carefully to this point, even if you do not agree with it," encourage active listening.

## Jargon

Professionals sometimes use jargon that prevents information from reaching others outside their field. The chairperson and others should ask for clarification of an unclear statement that uses jargon; however, no one should make fun of or demean users of jargon, because that creates a defensive response. A better technique is for the chairperson or other leader to rephrase the statement and ask whether the interpretation is correct.

## Problematic Styles of Participation

Because some group members are talkative and others are quiet, consideration should be given to all personal styles. However, a personal style should not interfere with the progress of the group (see chapter 5, "Work Styles" and "Learning Styles"). The different styles themselves are not problematic; they become problems when members are insensitive to their own style. When vocal individuals talk too much and quiet individuals withdraw, problems occur. Tempering personal style is the solution. For example, tempering the style of the overenthusiastic participator and enhancing the style of the excessively quiet participator is useful, and it models good behavior.

## Avoiding Group Conflict

Structuring the meetings and reports in the ways suggested in this book will reduce group conflict. There will still be conflicts, however, as passions and interests inevitably accompany community issues. Conflict is not always bad, though. Conflicts are like fires in the woods; smaller, more controlled fires are good because they burn off brush and allow new plants, or ideas, to grow. Large, raging fires are not good because the forest, or group, may burn completely.

## Managing Active Conflict

The following tips can be used to manage active conflict.

- *Recognize the benefits of limited conflicts.* The group does not have to call the fire department every time a small blaze erupts.
- *Get issues of conflict in the open early, because these issues do not go away.* Failing to address issues of conflict can lead to partisan

solutions, making community solutions harder to achieve. Bringing conflicts into the open early lowers tempers and increases the chance of obtaining a solution that gives everyone something of what they want.

- *Give opposing parties within the group a chance to resolve issues.* Getting issues in the open early allows subgroups of the opposing parties to reach a joint solution.
- *Use the community leader/organizer and consultants.* Sometimes the leader and consultants can meet with the different interests and come up with a win-win idea. The leader should be especially helpful when a situation has continued for some time and community members are locked into their positions.
- *Think win-win.* The chairperson especially has to think and espouse a win-win situation for everyone. It is not always possible for everyone to win, but the group culture should be structured so that everyone's interests are part of the solution.
- *Bracket problems.* Although bringing problems into the open early is good, bracketing, or setting a particular aspect of a problem aside should also be considered. Setting one part of a problem aside and working on other parts may allow the group, when it returns to the more difficult part of the problem, to find a solution.

### Lack of Conflict

Sometimes groups appear to have no conflict. However, it is more likely that conflict is being suppressed and defensive routines are being used. Possibly, a problem such as decision-avoidance psychosis, group think, the Abilene paradox, or the boiled-frog phenomenon (see chapter 1) has infected the group. Some conflict is necessary. Without it, important issues may be sidestepped.

## A USEFUL TEMPLATE FOR DISCUSSION

It is helpful to have a template to organize discussion. Several are available; the following pointers—adapted from Antony Jay's (1976) article "How to Run a Meeting" and the related training film *Meetings, Bloody*

*Meetings* (Video Arts, 1976)—are among the best. (see also, http://www.referenceforbusiness.com/encyclopedia/Cos-Des/Decision-Making.html)

- State and discuss the problem or issue at hand.
- Present various kinds of evidence.
- Discuss the evidence, determine what it proves, and see what people think about it.
- Make the decision and achieve closure.
- Implement and follow up.
- Follow up, evaluate, and refine the decision.
- Adjust the decision based on implementing experience.
- Revisit it at a future meeting if necessary.

## TECHNIQUES FOR DISCUSSION

Because the discussion is one of the most difficult parts of a group to manage, and addressing complex issues may seem impossible, it is helpful to have not only templates, but also a few techniques at hand. The following techniques can help improve the quality of discussions.

### Plan-Do-Check-Act Cycle

In total quality management, the plan-do-check-act cycle can be applied to the decision process. As issues approach, a plan is developed. Then decisions are made, and action ensues. The results of those decisions and actions are observed or checked. On the basis of this information, further action is taken if needed, and the cycle of improvement goes on.

### Six Thinking Hats

Sometimes it is difficult to bring different kinds of thinking or perspectives to a problem. Typically, someone plays the devil's advocate to elicit opinions and encourage people to think. Edward de Bono (1985) found a way to approach the problem. He invited people in groups to think of themselves as wearing hats of six different colors, each color being associated with a different kind of thinking.

- The *blue* hat suggests control and the organization of the thinking process.
- The *white* hat is neutral and concerned with objective facts and figures.
- The *yellow* hat is sunny, positive, optimistic, and hopeful.
- The *green* hat suggests creativity and new ideas.
- The *black* hat is gloomy and negative.
- The *red* hat suggests anger (seeing red), rage, and emotions.

Using this device, the chairperson does not have to say, "You are being too critical. Let's be more positive." An individual may resent that statement and begin a fight. Instead, the chairperson can say, "I have had a good bit of black hat (negative) thinking; perhaps I could have some from the green hat (creativity and new ideas)." In practice, hats are always referred to by their color and never by their function. The chairperson can ask someone to take off the black hat for a moment more easily than he or she can ask a person to stop being so negatively. (For fun, groups can make a set of colored hats available.)

There are other applications of this approach. One can, for example, ask community group members to play different roles than they typically do. Community group members, like other groups, tend to sit in the same seats and play the same roles. What they do not realize is that role redundancy actually limits their effectiveness, because other participants apply a discount rate to their ideas roughly proportional to the proportion of overparticipation that they perceive.

When a group moves through all hats in a single meeting, it is good to start with logic and positivity, and end with positivity. The sequenced list below may be helpful in this process.

1. The *blue* hat suggests control and the organization of the thinking process. It gets things going and outlines the process. Then go to factuality.
2. The *white* hat is neutral and concerned with objective facts and figures. Then go to positivity.
3. The *yellow* hat is sunny, positive, optimistic, and hopeful. Then go to creativity.
4. The *green* hat suggests creativity and new ideas. Then go to problems.

5. The *black* hat is gloomy and negative. Then go to feelings.
6. The *red* hat suggests feelings and emotions. Then return to positivity.
7. The *yellow* hat is sunny, positive, optimistic, and hopeful. Then return to the *blue* hat for decision and action, which *blue* facilitates.
8. The *blue* hat suggests control and the organization of the thinking process.

Alternatively, one can have a whole meting devoted to just one or a few of the hat perspectives. That tends to focus perspectives and get everyone on the same page.

## In-Principle Technique

The in-principle technique is useful when groups are seesawing between general ideas and details. It helps if the chairperson says at this time, "Let's agree in principle that this is the way we want to do this. We can work out the details by the next meeting." Avoid becoming entangled in details, such as group editing.

## Round-Robin Technique

The round-robin technique gets everyone's views in the open before discussion begins by going around the group and giving everyone who wants to a chance to speak. The chairperson can say, "To start this discussion, let's go one by one and share our preliminary views. We'll not discuss them now, just hear them as a way to get started." The chairperson should invite the less powerful members to begin the round robin, thus preventing members with power from dominating the group with their views.

## Sticky-Dot Voting Technique

The sticky-dot voting technique is a visual demonstration of group preferences and shows how extensive and deep those preferences are. For example, a community group has 26 goals, but it wants to have only five main goals for its vision statement. Each of the 26 alternatives is typed on separate sheets of paper, and the sheets are placed around the room. Group members are given five blue sticky dots and one gold dot. The members place their blue dots on the alternatives they feel are important.

They can put all five dots on one alternative, four on one and one on another alternative, one dot on five separate alternatives, or any other combination. This accounts for the depth of preference. Then, members put their gold dot on the alternative about which they feel most strongly. The dots are tallied, but it is usually clear which alternative has the most emphasis (the most blue dots) and which is considered the most serious (the most gold dots).

### Straw-Vote Technique

The straw-vote technique is a way to develop a preference ordering for the work of the community organizer or leader. For example, three or four issues come up in a meeting that need attention from the community leader. However, it is impossible to work on all of them before the next meeting. The chairperson can ask for a straw vote from the group about which issues the members think are most important. This vote provides guidance for the leader as to where his or her effort should be put.

## TECHNIQUES FOR DISCUSSING THE REPORT OF A SUBGROUP

### Problems --> Solutions

Frequently, a two-step approach is used in the decision-making process. First, a subgroup is assigned a problem and returns with an analysis and a recommendation. The members feel they have done a good job and seek approval. Second, the main group is asked to approve the old recommendation.

The main group, however, is often getting detailed information about the problem for the approach for the first time. As the members examine the recommendation, they are conscious of the need to do a good job and not approve the work of the subgroup without a thorough review. They often want to go over the recommendation in detail. The subgroup may feel as if their work is being questioned and, in a way, it is. This can result in a defensive response from the subgroup that inflames the main group and may convince them that the subgroup is trying to push something past them.

### Problem --> Options --> Recommendation

These questions and problems result from a lack of understanding about the task at hand and how to go about that task. Therefore, a change in presentation is needed. Instead of the two-step form of problem identification and recommendation, meeting masters recommend a three-step approach.

This three-step approach provides the group members with information they did not have before: the main alternatives or options that the subgroup worked through and the factors that resulted in the selection of one of them (see Appendix B for sample options menu). In this approach, the options are included in the presentation before the recommendation is made. Issues are presented in the following way:

- *The problem.* What problem is the group facing?
- *The options.* What are some options available to deal with the problem? (Three to four options are a good number with which to work.)
- *The recommendation.* Which of the options (or combination or sequence of options) does the subgroup recommend, and why?

The subgroup outlines these three points in a one-page executive summary. Then the chairperson or discussion leader invites the main group to examine the recommendation with four questions in mind:

- Was the logic in selecting the recommended option correct?
- Was the judgment correct? (Sometimes logic can be flawless, but judgment is faulty.)
- Have errors remained or crept in that the subgroup did not see? (This question has the potential to be negative, so do not begin with it.)
- Can the recommendation be improved, and if so, how?

If the group uses these questions, the discussion should proceed smoothly, and the overall community group and subgroup are focused on achieving the best decision possible.


CONCLUSION

Managing discussion is an important part of leadership in community process. Using the techniques in this chapter can lead to good discussion. Without good discussion, good decisions are rarely possible.

# Chapter 12
## The Effective Meeting: Managing Decisions

Good discussions are a necessary, but insufficient, condition for good decisions. Some groups still manage to avoid decisions, even when they are close to the decision point. The community leader needs help in assisting groups through the transition to decision.

### CLOSURE

Although a community group needs to make decisions, decision making is often avoided. Decision-avoidance psychosis robs the group of accomplishment. Over time, sometimes even a short time, group members conclude that nothing will happen and speak of the group's inability to make decisions with scorn and disdain. Though some individuals might have lobbied hard for decisions, they may also have contributed to the very pattern of which they now complain.

Decision avoidance illustrates another element to some people's approach to community-level decision making. If I cannot have my way, no one will get their way either. Such a view reflects a "zero sum" approach: I win, or lose. The idea of an all-win, or a community win, does not seem to be part of their thinking.

There are many other reasons why people avoid making decisions. One, just mentioned, has to do with not wanting to lose. If one person gets what he or she wants, somebody else loses. In close communities, people see each other frequently; winners and losers may have to face each other. Losers may be embarrassed; winners may feel guilty. It is one thing to face someone once at a meeting; it is another to see him or her every day. Sometimes it may seem best to step back from a decision and do nothing.

Unfortunately, the nondecision decision is something. As a popular poster says, "Not to decide is to decide." In other words, inaction or delay is another form of decision. Sometimes it is the right one. However, it is always better to affirmatively decide on delay than to drift into the decision.

In addition, decisions often are avoided because people perceive them as permanent; the fear that decisions cannot be modified often causes decision-avoidance psychosis. Group members often wonder, as they approach a decision, what the consequences will be if the decision is disastrous. The chairperson must stress, and members must understand, that decisions are rarely that fateful. Although decisions may not be reversed, they can be adjusted, smoothed, and pointed in ways that incorporate new information and perspectives. Decisions often undergo review and improvement. Keep in mind, though, that this approach can be pushed too far. Group members do not want to review decisions constantly.

## DECISION RULES

Meeting masters learn the slow process of how groups come to decisions, and they know things that others do not. For example, individuals in a group propose an action and are criticized and faulted; it is clear that the proposed action is not what the group wants to do. However, meeting masters can listen to a discussion, review the progress, and suggest a course of action. Frequently, group members respond by saying the meeting master's suggestion is the right course of action. What has happened?

This ability of meeting masters to hone in on the key issue or problem is an important skill, because the cacophony of group participation, the disparity of views, and strongly held and opposing positions may not seem to allow for a resolution. How does a resolution that satisfies most of the people in the room happen? The answer involves knowledge about decision rules and the process of decision crystallization, discussed later in this chapter.

Decision rules—norms from society—are decision legitimizing, and they are accepted as authoritative. In most decision-making groups, there are five decision rules that cause conflict: extensive decision rule, intensive decision rule, involvement rule, expert rule, and power rule. The operation of any rule alone would yield a different set of results than the simultaneous operation of all five. Meeting masters know the decision rules and orchestrate solutions that blend several of the rules simultaneously.

Basically, all groups want to know about five things as they come to decisions. First, they want to know about the breadth of preference. What do most people think? Second, they want to know who feels strongly, how strongly they feel, and whether some accommodation can be made for their feelings. Third, groups want to know what the people involved (usually those who have to pay or carry something out) feel. Fourth, it is important to understand the state of expertise on the matter. What do the scientists and lawyers think? What do the most experienced people in the room think? What do the travel planners think? And finally, they want to know about power. We are always interested in what the boss, or the most influential community or family member, thinks.

Although we all are aware of these rules, not all groups weigh each rule equally. As you think about decision making in your community—or family or workplace—think about what proportion of weight the group places on each. If they were all rated equally, each weight would be 25 percent. But, of course, they are not. The three that any particular group weighs the most creates the decision culture of that particular group. Let's look at each of the rules in a little detail.

Extensive Decision Rule

The extensive decision rule is the most popular, or at least most public, rule. It refers to one person, one vote, and it tests the breadth of preference. Each individual has the same say, and that some individuals feel strongly about an issue and others do not is irrelevant in the application of the extensive decision rule.

This rule has been used by everyone. Most groups, however, recognize that there are other rules on which a decision could be based. The extensive decision rule is inadequate unless the group feels that other decision rules, and the results that the application of those rules would generate, have been addressed.

### Intensive Decision Rule

People feel more strongly about some things than others. Depth of preference is never addressed by the extensive decision rule. Groups seek to find out who feels strongly about which issues and, if possible, make some accommodation. Depth of preference is important. Recall the discussion of the sticky-dot voting technique; if a member feels strongly about an alternative, he or she puts all sticky dots on that alternative. In the intensive decision rule, group members try to discover who has strong feelings, so that they can take their strength of preference into account when making a decision.

### Involvement Rule

Most decisions have implementation actions, and sometimes people in the decision-making process are involved in the implementation or have preferences about how the implementation should be carried out. Those who are involved in the implementation usually have more say in the decision than those who are not. In most households, a simple example of this rule is the statement, "The one who has to make dinner gets to pick dinner."

### Expert Rule

In many areas (for example, medical care) some issues are known best by experts, and making a decision is not as simple as voting, because the members of the group may not have enough technical expertise. Furthermore, it may not always be clear whether an issue has been addressed by an expert or how convinced that expert might be on the issue. Groups should be aware of what experts are saying with regard to an issue, even if some individuals might not agree with the experts.

### Power Rule

In business, the power rule is expressed in the question, "What does the boss think?" In community groups, power is often expressed through social prestige or high occupational position. As a result, powerful individuals in the community have influence, and people want to know what they think.

### Definition of Consensus

When most groups talk about consensus, they have only a vague idea of what is really meant by it. Using all five decision rules, we can arrive at a definition. When a proposed decision meets and can be shown to meet these five rules, consensus has been achieved. The difficulty is that decisions often have to be made on the spot, so knowledge of the decision rules is not always enough. Using the rules well becomes a key skill.

## DECISION CRYSTALLIZATION

Meeting masters help groups make decisions through a process called decision crystallization. *Decision crystallization* involves acting on behalf of the group decision rather than one's own interests; it involves taking risks, being opposed, stepping back, and engaging in a give-and-take process of constructing a decision. It begins after a period of discussion and goes through rounds of discussion, summative reflection, action hypothesis, vocalization and action legitimization, and discussion refocus.

### Rounds of Discussion

Meeting masters invite discussion on a topic by asking questions, but not contributing much of their own views. They might express an occasional preference, but they do more listening than talking early in the decision process.

Meeting masters pay attention to rounds of discussion, which occur when each person has made one comment (it could be at the end of a round-robin episode, for example) or when everyone who wants to make a contribution during that round has done so. There is usually a pause at this time, and it is vital that the chairperson or other leader begins the process of crystallization at the end of the first round of discussion, before individuals go into a second, repetitive round. A second round of discussion is not held unless some degree of closure has been achieved after the first round.

### Summative Reflection

At the end of the round of discussion, meeting masters begin a summative reflection—a summary of where the group stands on a topic during the decision-making process. This reflection allows the group to hear what it has been saying. Many individuals may not remember what everyone else has said during the discussion, which can be a problem if no one is taking time to organize and present in a structured way the ideas that have been discussed. Therefore, summative reflection is an organized approach to the discussion, not just a repeat of what individuals have said. As the chairperson or community leader listens, he or she should be organizing the discussion, on paper or in his or her head, and feeding it back to the group.

### Action Hypothesis/Proposal

When summative reflection has been completed, the action hypothesis phase begins. A leader would say, "The following seems to be a reasonable course of action." This is how the Abilene paradox (see chapter 1) is avoided. Someone has taken it on himself or herself to voice a suggested action. The hope is that the alternative will be presented and legitimized in such a way as to make it palatable to the group members and thus stimulate agreement.

### Vocalization and Action Legitimization

For a group decision to be made, action must be vocalized and legitimized. Vocalization involves the interaction between the person who speaks, working on behalf of the group's interests, and the group members, with their different interests, depth of involvement, expertise, and power.

The immediate next step after vocalization is action—action legitimization, during which decision rules are put to work. A chairperson may say, "Where should we go for lunch today? The restaurant across the street would be a good place (the action hypothesis), because (the legitimization) most people seem to find that acceptable (extensive decision rule addressed). It has a salad bar for those who do not want to eat meat (intensive decision rule), and John doesn't care where he goes for lunch (involvement rule). They have a new low-fat burger (expert rule), and the boss doesn't care where we spend our lunch money (power)." At that point, group members give assent with phrases such as, "Sounds like a great idea," and "Fine with me."

## Discussion Refocus

At the decision point, the leader refocuses the group discussion on the next issue, the next step of its business. This refocus process is subtle, but on reflection, individuals who use these techniques will see new methods for group decision making. The risk is that individuals will receive criticism for suggesting an action hypothesis (going on to the next issue). Risks taken on behalf of advancing the group (as long as they are not a cover for advancing individual interests) and recognized by the group are rewarded with increased group influence. The process goes on until the entire decision is constructed.

## When a Second Round Is Needed

What if people do not agree? Suppose the discussion does not go as smoothly as suggested? After the initial advancement of an action hypothesis, the reaction of the group is negative. It was still useful to advance the action hypothesis, because during discussion the group learned that the action was not what they wanted to do. In that case, the leader or chairperson should suggest a second round of discussion but ask people to express preferences that differ from those they have already expressed. People should be invited to stretch their preferences and think of new ideas, approaches, and opportunities. If this request is not made, the second round of discussion will be a repeat of the first; everyone will restate what they have already shared.

After the second round of discussion, the process of summative reflection, action hypothesis, and vocalization and action legitimization is repeated. This time, however, the process is more complicated. The chairperson or leader should keep the array of ideas from rounds one and two together and synthesize opinions from the two rounds. For particularly difficult issues that require three, four, or five rounds of discussion, decisions are a possible but daunting task. Using this process, however, discussion progresses—builds—toward a decision.

## DECISION SCULPTING

When all the smaller parts of the decision have been made, the group steps back and engages in the final step in the process. Decision sculpting involves looking at the decision that has been constructed and assessing whether anything has been left out, problems have been created, or adjustments and alterations are needed. Once the group members are satisfied that the decision looks balanced and appeals to a variety of interests, they can move ahead.

## CONCLUSION

The process of managing groups toward decisions is complicated, and exercising community leadership while managing toward decisions is even more complex. Fortunately, there are techniques and skills that help accomplish this process. No one is born with these skills; however, individuals who develop them can help a community group make decisions that work.

# Chapter 13
## Managing Assessments

Community management and leadership in the 21st century is results driven. Businesses, government organizations, and nonprofit organizations are conscious of the need to accomplish tasks. This same drive to achieve results occurs in both the volunteer sector and at the board level. Individuals are eager to give their time for community purposes but are unwilling to waste it. If a community leadership program cannot show that it can achieve goals and make progress such that the individuals in the process can experience and enjoy the achievements, there will be a high rate of participant dropout. For this reason, assessment is a crucial component of community planning activities.

### ASSESSMENT RATHER THAN EVALUATION

I use the word "assessment" rather than the more common term "evaluation," to avoid the judgmental overtone that evaluation carries. Following an assessment, a group may require decision and action: Improve this meeting, change this process, reevaluate that program, and so on. But the process of reviewing and assessing community activities, procedures, programs, and plans works best if it does not, in itself, contain judgments, conclusions, or recommendations. Furthermore, it is wise to determine the recipient of the assessment in advance of establishing the protocol and carrying out the assessment. What community organization receives the report on which calls for decision and action might be based? Making that clear at the beginning clarifies expectations for everyone involved in the process.

## PURPOSES OF ASSESSMENT

Assessment serves several purposes. First, assessments are a method to review work and determine how to improve a process or procedure. Second, assessments (or, more accurately, the knowledge that an assessment protocol is in place) motivate individuals to do their best work. Group members, knowing that their performance will be assessed, approach tasks with heightened responsibility, attention, and focus. This prospect of an assessment improves performance in much the same way as reporting weight at a medical appointment encourages control of eating habits. Care must be taken, though, to ensure the assessment design is not so elaborate that it is unusable or off-putting.

Third, groups facing an assessment, whether as assessors or assessees, inevitably ask, "Assessment of what?" The "of what" drives *conceptualization*—setting of goals and objectives, the achievement of which will be assessed. Good assessment requires preset goals and a set of metrics. That does not mean additional goals cannot be added, or metrics adjusted, but it does mean that one must begin with goals and measures already in place.

Fourth, assessment is a constructive, authentic way to involve community members and participants in community growth initiatives. Furthermore, community-based assessment often provides an effective structure for an assessment process. Although community members will participate as respondents, they may also, in the community-based assessment model, help design and carry out the assessment as well.

Finally, developing and implementing an assessment protocol sends a message to the community: A group that evaluates its work must be serious about it. An assessment process can even aid recruitment of new group members because it communicates seriousness and commitment.

## TYPES OF ASSESSMENT: OVERVIEW

The Minnesota Department of Health (n.d.) publishes a useful table of popular assessment styles, reproduced here (see Table 13-1). Note that it uses the term evaluation, but assessment works just as well. And, although

## TABLE 13-1: Five Approaches to Assessment/Evaluation

| | |
|---|---|
| **Process** (also called "methods") | Process evaluation examines the procedures and tasks involved in implementing a program. This type of evaluation also can look at the administrative and organizational aspects of the program. Process evaluation monitors the program to ensure feedback during the course of the program. |
| **Impact** (also called "outcome objectives") | Impact evaluation is the most comprehensive of the four evaluation types. It is desirable because it focuses on the long-range results of the program and changes or improvements in health status as a result. However, impact evaluations are rarely possible because they are frequently costly and involve extended commitment. Also, the results often cannot be directly related to the effects of an activity or program because of other (external) influences on the target audience, which occur over time. Information obtained from an impact study may include:<br><br>• Changes in morbidity and mortality<br>• Changes in absenteeism from work<br>• Long-term maintenance of desired behavior<br>• Rate or recidivism<br>[Ed. note: These are health care examples from their posting. We could easily substitute community examples, such as:<br>• Levels of community participation<br>• Community/neighborhood appearance<br>• School attendance<br>• Reduction in juvenile "incidents"<br>• More homeless services<br>• Better community policing] |
| **Outcome** (also called "bridging objectives") | Outcome evaluation is used to obtain descriptive data on a project and to document short-term results. Task-focused results are those that describe the output of the activity (for example, the number of public inquiries received as a result of a public service announcement). Short-term results describe the immediate effects of the project on the target audience (for example, percentage of the target audience showing increased awareness of the subject). Information that can result from an outcome evaluation includes the following:<br><br>• Knowledge and attitude changes<br>• Expressed intentions of the target audience<br>• Short-term or intermediate behavior shifts<br>• Policies initiated or other institutional changes made |
| **Formative** | Formative evaluation, including pretesting, is designed to assess the strengths and weaknesses or materials or campaign strategies before implementation. Formative research tailors the program to the target audience. Messages or products are tested by a small group before they are implemented on a large scale. This type of evaluation permits necessary revisions before the full effort goes forward. Its basic purpose is to maximize the change for program success before the activity starts. |
| **Summative** | Any combination measurements and judgments that permit conclusions to be drawn about impact, outcome, or benefits of a program or method. |

its examples are health-oriented, community objectives can be met with each of these assessment styles.

## TYPES OF ASSESSMENT: MEETINGS, DECISIONS, AND IMPLEMENTATION

Because community growth is so often advanced through meetings and decisions, this section focuses on tools for assessing meetings and decisions. The first type of assessment is simply a review of each meeting, which helps the individuals who manage the meeting have a sense of what is happening and what needs to be improved. The second is the decision audit, which considers the range of decisions and assesses the overall decision performance of the community organization or meetings in question. The third is the decision autopsy, which examines particular good and poor decisions in depth. The fourth is implementation analysis, a review of how well the decision was actually carried out. However, great outcomes (GO) are not only the result of producing good meetings and building great decisions, but also the result of implementation. Great positive outcomes follow the formula:

$$GO = \text{Great Decisions} \times \text{Great Implementation}$$

Of course, poor decisions can be "salvaged" by creative implementation, and great decisions can be sabotaged (deliberately and accidentally) by implementation problems.

### Meeting Assessment

After a meeting ends, participants should be asked how they feel about it. One simple, but effective, method for this check-in is the keep-stop-start (KSS) approach. Group members should prepare lists with the following information and give the lists to the community leader or chairperson.

Keep: What about this meeting should we keep doing?
Stop: What about this meeting should be discontinued?
Start: Are there things in this meeting you did not see that we should start?

The leader and chairperson should use the suggestions received to adjust future content or process of the meeting.

In the meeting assessment phase, participants assess process rather than goals or decisions. They should observe for indicators of good process, for example, satisfaction with the process even though any particular participant did not get his or her way, exactly. Participants should have the feeling of authenticity, the sense that the meeting they were in was the "real" meeting, not some political construct that had a foreordained result.

### Decision Audit

Because decisions are the work product of the group, they should be reviewed periodically and considered from a task, rather than process, perspective. The group can conduct a decision audit (as well as a decision autopsy, discussed later) according to a fixed time schedule, or on an annual basis.

The frequency of the audit depends on the turbulence of the group's environment. In a fast-paced environment, the audit cycle should be about every six months or more because, by the time a group in a volatile environment discovers it has been making wrong decisions, it is often too late to alter course. In a tranquil environment, an audit every 18 to 24 months may be acceptable. If a group is seeking to change meeting technology within a slow-moving system, quick audit cycles will reinforce members' efforts even though the environment is not turbulent.

During a decision audit, members *do* make judgments. As readers will see, decisions are graded from A to F, because some actually *are* better than others. The decision audit requires a good minute-taking system. For the group to review its decisions (perhaps 20 percent of them), they should be easily accessible. If the minutes have been kept according to the content minutes pattern, decisions will be shaded or boxed, and easy to extract. A 20 percent sample then can be easily identified for audit if the person collating the decisions begins in a random location and chooses every fifth decision thereafter. If decisions are difficult to extract from the minutes, the audit may be over as soon as it starts. If the decisions are opaque or unclear, or if the keeper of the minutes cannot find the minutes, group members probably are not sure what happened either. Once decisions are identified, though, they should be listed, and one to three individuals should grade them. Grading criteria of A to F are straightforward:

- *A decision.* An all-win in which all stakeholders are ahead (although they do not have to all be equally ahead). When people say after a meeting, "That was a good decision," they are referring to a decision in which everybody came out ahead. If this were a stock portfolio, all of our stocks would have increased in value, although not equally.

- *B decision.* A plus–minus decision in which some stakeholders lose but a larger number of stakeholders gain. On balance, the decision leaves the group ahead of where it started. Perhaps the group decided on a merger, which reduces two executive positions to one. The combined efficiencies and effectiveness of the new operation, however, make the sacrifice of personnel worthwhile. In our stock portfolio, some stocks lost money while others gained, but the average gain is on the plus side of the ledger.

- *C decision.* A null decision that produced gains and losses with the net result of zero. Some people gained and some lost; the system, however, is no farther ahead than it was before the decision.

- *D decision.* This is the opposite of a B decision. Some gains and some losses resulted from the decision, but there may have been heavy losses in one area that are not overcome by positive gains. Deming (1982) termed these "incalculable losses." In our stock portfolio, the overall effect is entered on the negative side of the ledger.

- *F decision.* Sometimes called the nuclear-war or all-lose decision. Every stakeholder is behind where they were before the decision was made. In our stock portfolio, every stock lost value.

Reviewers then sum up the grades and present a grade distribution and brief discussion. Although this system is useful, there are other ways to rate decisions. It is the process of decision analysis, not necessarily the analysis protocol, that is important. The decision review meeting should receive careful attention. The decision audit is not a witch hunt; every effort should be made not to seek guilty parties. If decision making has not gone well, the group should make an effort to determine (perhaps using a decision autopsy, discussed later) what the problems are and how they can be corrected.

Discussion topics stemming from the audit should be prefaced with a statement that the decisions were something common to the entire group; if decisions were made in error, everyone made them, and if benefits were attained, everyone deserves the glory. Emphasis on team effort and team spirit is essential to make the decision audit work.

Decision Autopsy

The *decision autopsy* is a more detailed disassembly of an A decision and an F decision. In a decision autopsy, reviewers conduct an in-depth analysis of what went right (and how to continue successes) and what went wrong (and how to prevent future failures). For both psychological and theoretical reasons, it is important to examine an A decision and an F decision.

From a psychological perspective, analyzing both A and F decisions creates the good news-bad news scenario that is beneficial in examining problems. As we learn from conducting performance appraisals, it is important to say, "Here are some things that are going right and that we should continue. In addition, here are some things that are not going well, and we need to look at them in detail and figure out together how we can improve them." Most people feel defensive when things they are associated with go wrong. They may protest, "It's not our fault" and avoid coming to grips with their part in the problem. That resistance is lessened if pointing out problem areas can be balanced by highlighting successful aspects of performance, or of a decision. The overall goal is to improve the community group's decision-making grade, not to develop fault-finding norms.

From a theoretical perspective, most groups (and individuals, for that matter) do not learn well from success or failure. First, they do not have reflective periods that permit a close examination of the recent past and an understanding of the dynamics that drive them. Second, they find successes and failures difficult to learn from because successes make them feel good, and they therefore want to keep pressing the pedal for more treats. Failures, though, make them feel bad, and they more often than not lapse into defensive avoidance, failing to truly examine the "failure" or seek knowledge and guidance from it.

The idea is to find out what went right in the positive case, and what went wrong in the negative case. Thus, avoidance of "blame-storming" is essential. A decision autopsy is not an excuse to "pin-the-tail-on-the-donkey" but rather an opportunity to explore the processes and systems that led to greatness or failure.

And it is important to stress here that results may not be driven by the same factors. As noted earlier, everyone makes great and poor decisions. But it is not always the case that the poor decision is caused by factors diametrically opposed to those that prompted the good one, although that is sometimes the case. ("I usually think things through, but this time I did not," for example.) Rather, different factors may be at work in motivating a good or bad decision. Thus, a simplistic "We will never do *that* again" will not yield much insight. Members need to give in-depth consideration to the root causes of successful and unsuccessful decision making.

### Implementation Analysis

Great outcomes (GOs) are not only the result of producing good meetings and building great decisions, but also the result of implementation. Thus, GOs follow the formula GOs = great decisions × great implementation. Although poor decisions can be salvaged by creative implementation, and great decisions can be sabotaged (deliberately and accidentally) by ineffective implementation, it is nevertheless important to understand how well or poorly the decision has been acted on. The lack of proper implementation can doom excellent plans, just as creative implementation can save rotten ones. One good approach to analyzing the implementation of a decision is the after-action review or after-action report. A simple Google search produces thousands of samples of each, and Wikipedia (see http://en.wikipedia.org/wiki/After_action_report) lists the following elements of an after-action report:

- Overview
- Goals and objectives
- Analysis of outcomes
- Analysis of the performance shown on critical tasks
- Summary
- Lessons learned *(This item is my addition.)*
- Recommendations

## CONCLUSION

Assessment is a crucial part of the community leadership and organizing process. It is especially important in community work, because outcomes are hard to define and measure. These assessment measures are not in-depth, but they are designed to communicate to group members that their actions are important, have consequences, and will be assessed. These measures give everyone the opportunity to shape the ongoing process and do so in the light of the preferences of the entire group.

# Part Four
## Rewards of Community Leadership

Communities need leadership now more than ever. Citizens are, if anything, starved for leadership, which is, perhaps, why fringe groups seem so attractive to some. Others retreat—cocooning into homes and interacting only with themselves and a few family members. They work at home, shop from home, watch videos at home, and have food delivered. Both these results, and others, occur in part because community connection cannot be accomplished smoothly and easily. In the absence of community connection, we are drawn into groups that look like communities but are actually cults. Or we give up on community completely.

Cohesive, caring communities are vital to an outstanding quality of life. But like anything else, the value of community must be worth the investment. Community leadership is the force that creates functioning communities and helps members build value that is worth the investment they make in a community. Functioning communities, in turn, can be connecting and caring groups, to which members can give their allegiance. But communities must be run well; those characterized by ineffective process; rancorous, endless meetings; useless results; and rampant partisanship will soon lose the commitment and participation of their members.

Many issues divide American communities (and all communities), and it is always difficult to build bridges within and among communities. Over and above the normal cleavages in communities, the climate in the United States, both before and during the 9/11 era, seems especially contentious and ideologically driven. Community solutions seem to pale before individualistic solutions, and much of American society resembles an orchestra with no conductor—everyone is tooting their own horn, so to speak.

The role of *maestro* is the aim of a successful community organizer and leader. A maestro works within and outside the system to help communities small and large move from a "me" orientation to a "we" orientation. A maestro creates solutions that address breadth of preference, depth of preference, involvement, expertise, and power (see chapter 12, "Decision Rules").

Community leadership and organization are often contentious, problematic, and thankless roles. Much is expected, often for little reward or appreciation. But much personal satisfaction comes from helping loose, ambiguous collectivities come together as effective organizational systems. Working with a community to grow and to accomplish all-win solutions is the reward inherent in community organization and leadership.

Two additional steps will encourage organizers and leaders in their work. One, discussed in chapter 14, is to develop a conceptual understanding of the complexities of the leader's role and its different elements. The second, addressed in chapters 15 and 16, is to grow the capacity for leadership—learning to move from a good community organizer and leader to a great one by embracing servant leadership and building a legacy.

# Chapter 14
## Being a Successful Community Leader and Organizer

Being a successful community organizer and leader involves attention to and cultivation of the seven Cs (Tropman & Wooten, 2010). The 7C approach is a taxonomy that organizes the seven areas to which community organizers and leaders attend and in which they need to work:

1. Characteristics
2. Competencies
3. Collaborations
4. Crucibles
5. Conditions
6. Contexts
7. Change

Numbers 1 to 4 are personal features, or properties, of the individual organizer or leader. Number 5, conditions, refers to the agency or organization within which the community organizer and leader works or participates. Number 6, contexts, calls attention to the culture and structure of the environment, both micro-, or community, environment and the macrostate, -national, and -global environments within which a leader works. Number 7, change, focuses on types and rates of change and how successful leaders and organizers manage them.

## THE 7C TAXONOMY

### Areas

*Characteristics.* Characteristics can include personal elements of the successful community organizer and leader. These could be physical characteristics such as race, ethnicity, gender; or temperamental characteristics, such as a Myers Briggs type or a general disposition. Because communities are diverse, a diversity of community leadership is always appropriate. Community leaders and organizers are often working in fluid situations with many stakeholders. For these reasons the community leadership needs to represent a diversity of characteristics. One implication of this perspective is that community leadership needs to be "grown" or constantly developed (see chapter 15). Although leadership development is an ongoing challenge for all systems, it is especially important for communities.

Community organizers and leaders are aware of their personal characteristics and how they may facilitate, enhance, or retard their ability to work effectively with a community. Because they are aware, community organizers and leaders can strategically and tactically use these characteristics (some of which cannot be changed) to maximize their utility and minimize their negative effect within a community.

*Competencies.* Competencies refer to the package of knowledge and skills that the successful community leader and organizer needs. The knowledge is, in part, theoretical and, in part, practical: The leader understands, at minimum, theories of problems common to communities (lack of cohesion, capability, or competence) and models of community change (strategies of community development, action, and planning). She or he also grasps social science perspectives—drawn from anthropology, economics, and sociology, among others—on communities and community behavior. Practically speaking, the leader or organizer possesses local knowledge. Local knowledge requires an understanding of how theoretical perspectives apply to the community-at-hand, but it also involves knowing the community's history, values, local lore, elites, and participants.

Skill, however, is the ability to activate this theoretical and practical knowledge so that it works on behalf of the community. A Google search of the term "leadership skills" yields thousands of results. Lists of necessary skills include such items as communications and public relations, listening, marketing, broad interpersonal and emotional intelligence, technical training (meeting management, event planning, information technology, to name a few) as well as negotiation and conflict management skills. Successful community leaders and organizers not only have a broad range of competencies, but also develop and improve them on an ongoing basis.

*Collaborations.* Successful community organizers and leaders have a "board of advisers" so to speak, individuals with whom they consult and on whom they rely for assistance and insight. They tend to collaborate with a diverse and varied group of people who offer both support and challenge.

*Crucibles.* Crucibles are formative experiences, positive or not-so-positive, that imprint the community organizer or leader with distinctive perspectives and approaches. Successful workers are aware of these traits; they use them, but are not used by them.

*Conditions.* Conditions refer to the properties of the community itself, its structure (formal and informal), elite and opinion-leader structure, political structure, and range of relevant governments (among them sewer districts, education districts, and so on). It also includes awareness of community cultures and subcultures, and possible points of tension and cooperation within and among them.

*Contexts.* Successful community organizers and leaders need to relate well to the two general contexts in which they and their community (from which they draw resources and to which they provide leadership) exist. The local context includes grantors, funding sources, donors, foundations, journalists, competitor and supportive entities, and other related organizations that are "in town." It also includes the local regulatory system. The extracommunity context includes influential professional and political figures and state and national agencies.

Regarding context, the successful community leader and organizer works on two fronts. On the first front, the leader helps the community adjust itself to both developing (intracommunity) changes and to incoming (extracommunity) changes, increasing the community's nimbleness quotient. On the second front, the leader helps the community exert influence to shape those contexts, strengthening its advocacy quotient.

*Change.* Change refers to the speed at which change is occurring in any of the six other Cs. In contemporary Western society, change is probably happening at the pace of a Web year, approximately three months, rather than a calendar year. To make matters worse, change does not occur at the same rate or in the same magnitude in all Cs. This asynchronicity produces both cultural lag (norms fall behind structural advances) and structural lag (structures fall behind cultural advances). Sayles and Chandler (1993) asserted that the successful community leader must step above the fray, organizing and leading proactive, fundamental change in community missions and processes. Those who lead communities effectively through change must demonstrate skill in managing problems at the right time and in the right sequence, setting and changing decision-making criteria as necessary, and increasing the sense of urgency when needed.

## THE LONGER VIEW: STRUCTURES AND PATTERNS

The 7C taxonomy allows us to locate pieces of the literature in a "place," that is, to sort them by emphasis. Such placement does not indicate a right or wrong, but it does call attention to what a piece of literature might be missing, or what it might need to include to present a fuller picture of community leadership and organization. For example, the well-known "Level 5 Leadership" concept (Collins, 2005) emphasizes two dimensions: humility and fierce resolve. Viewed through the 7C lens, level 5 leadership concentrates primarily on characteristics. Goleman's (2006) emphasis on emotional intelligence focused on competence (intra- and interpersonal skill) as did Hochschild's (2003) discussion in the *Managed Heart*. In *Beyond Rational Management,* Quinn (1988) stressed organizational conditions. He listed four types of organizational subculture—clan, bureaucracy, market, and advocacy—that call attention to default styles of organizational behavior and expectations. Prahalad's (2005) *Bottom of the Pyramid* stressed contexts and the pressures and opportunities that they present communities and leaders. Tichy and Devanna's (1986) *Transformational Leader* stressed change as a key element in organizational analysis. Baker (1994) emphasized collaboration in *Networking Smart,* though he focused more on networking for personal position, rather than networking as an organizational resource. Crisis management literature such as *When It Hits the Fan* (Myers, 1987) fits into the crucibles category, as does literature considering early life experiences of executive leaders.

## CONCLUSION

The 7C structure can serve as a roadmap for understanding vital facets of leadership, areas that leaders need to influence, and factors that influence leaders. Successful community leadership and organizing depends on both competence and reflection. It is hard to be a reflective community leader and organizer if one is overwhelmed with leadership material from so many differing perspectives. The 7C structuring and patterning of leadership literature allows one to read and reflect systematically, to see the parts, the whole, and the interaction within and among those parts. This, in turn, helps leaders "grow" their leadership.

# Chapter 15
## Growing Your Leadership

Amy Chua, Yale professor and author of the controversial book *Battle Hymn of the Tiger Mother* (2011), argued that nothing is fun until you are good at it. How do you get good at community organization and leadership? Malcolm Gladwell (2008), in *Outliers*, argued that practice, lots of practice, is the key to expertise. He cites the 10,000-hour rule (about five years of conventional full-time work) as a measure of how much practice produces expertise. Successful community organizers and leaders practice by *doing* leadership and community organization. But I would add to the Chua–Gladwell recipe that practice must be mindful and reflective, not simply rote. Practice that nurtures expertise is a cycle of doing, reflecting, analyzing, improving, and redoing, similar to Deming's (1982) plan-do-check-act cycle.

### CONSTANT LEARNING

This means that we are always "in school," that learning is no longer relegated to the early part of the life cycle, but that lifelong learning is the norm. We are always refining and improving our leadership skills. To paraphrase Collins (2005), it is good to be good, but better to be great, and to accept the ongoing challenge of staying great and becoming even greater.

The 7C template provides leaders a structure that helps them grow while thinking and working through situations. Successful community organizers and leaders need to review their dispositions and behaviors within each of these vectors to ensure growth. Taking the time to review and reflect on disposition and behavior is the difference between having five years of experience or one year of experience, five times (also known as the Groundhog Day effect).

Growth, refinement, and comprehensiveness within each vector are vital to the increasing competence levels of successful community leaders and organizers. In their book *Mind over Machine,* Dreyfus and Dreyfus (1986) identified five levels of skill acquisition and display that span a staircase of competence from novice to master. Briefly, an individual learning any new competency is a novice, moves to beginner status, and then arrives at the level of journeyperson, where most individuals are in most competencies. Experts are high-level journeypeople who are specialists in a few areas. Master leaders and organizers are exceptional and are recognized as such by community members, coprofessionals, and others. They are seamless in their performance, good at big picture and small details, good at visioning and execution, and virtuosos at the disciplined use of self in relationship.

In my opinion, though, Dreyfus and Dreyfus stopped one step early. Master, or virtuoso, leaders emphasize personal accomplishment and skill. The maestro leader, though, possesses not only preeminent personal mastery, but also exceptional ability to bring others together in teamwork. Masters are not always leaders. Maestros are. The metaphor of orchestra conductor as leader is apt here. Indeed, conductor Roger Nierenberg (2009), in his book *Maestro,* discussed executive leadership in just this way. So, average leaders can be journeypeople, beginners, or novices, because everyone starts somewhere. But they do not have to stay where they start.

## THE SKILL STAIRCASE: FROM NOVICE TO MAESTRO

*Successful Community Leader and Organizer Level 1: Novice Skills*

- Performance slow and jerky
- Attention to rules and facts
- Works with the book in hand
- Heavy learner

*Problem: Receives little reinforcement from the task.*

*Successful Community Leader and Organizer: Level 2, Beginner Skills*
- Performance faster and smoother
- Begins rule fade (acting automatically)
- Patterns not mentioned in rules
- Uses book less frequently
- Learner

*Problem: Embarrassments to self and others.*

*Successful Community Leader and Organizer:*
*Level 3, Journeyperson Skills*
- Performance average in terms of speed and smoothness
- Rule fade mostly complete
- Selecting most important cues
- Calculated, educated risk taking
- Uses book only for exceptions
- Learner/teacher

*Problem: May think this is the end of development and growth.*

*Successful Community Leader and Organizer: Level 4, Expert Skills*
- Performance becomes fluid
- Rule fade is complete
- Calculation and rationality diminish
- No plan is permanent
- Attention shifts with cues
- Holistic, intuitive grasp
- Can write the book
- Teacher

*Problem: Possible overuse of default skill because it comes so easily; may also not realize average or below average skill in other areas.*

*Successful Community Leader and Organizer:*
*Level 5, Virtuoso/Master Skills*
- Performance is seamless
- Works at exactly the right speed; appears effortless
- Understands the deep structure of the effort
- Possesses a holistic recognition of cues

- Performance is solid, confident, and sure
- Deep understanding of task
- Trusts self and the process, lets process flow, enters as needed
- Works beyond the book

*Problem: Finding, arranging, and managing access to the master's knowledge and self.*

*Successful Community Leader and Organizer: Level 6, Maestro Skills*

- Goes beyond self-performance
- Orchestrates team performance
- Lifts others up
- Practices contributory leadership
- Practices servant leadership

*Problem: Wisely selecting those vital few leadership and organizing assignments where contributions have the most influence.*

## CONCLUSION

Collins's (2005) model level 5 leadership is grounded in humility and fierce resolve. I argue, though, that there are six levels. The last is not only the management of ego (humility), but also specific ability to orchestrate the work of others, of all levels, for community betterment (fierce resolve). Reflective practice, improving your own practice, and growing your leadership through these levels is still not the end of the leadership-development road. The successful community organizer and leader also cultivates new leaders, with an eye toward diversifying the leadership pool and creating leadership bench strength.

# Chapter 16
## Developing Fresh Community Leadership

The responsibilities of successful community leaders and organizers do not end, though, with personal reflection, self-development, and movement to maestro status. The continual charge and challenge of successful leaders is to develop new community leadership, and to do so in ways that blend the ambition for personal achievement and accomplishment with the desire to develop a communitywide solution to community problems in a timely and creative fashion. In developing fresh community leadership, several goals and principles are useful to keep in mind.

## SERVANT LEADERSHIP

The community leader ultimately strives to cultivate servant leadership. Servant leadership represents the meld of personal and community ambition. It begins with the natural feeling that one wants to serve first; conscious choice then nurtures one to aspire to lead. That person differs sharply from one who aspires to lead first, perhaps because of the need to assuage an unusual drive for power or material acquisition. The leader-first and the servant-first are two extreme types. Between them there are shadings and blends that are part of the infinite variety of human nature.

Larry C. Spears (Leider & Spears, 2009), former president and chief executive of the Robert K. Greenleaf Center for Servant Leadership, extracted 10 elements that are central to the development of a servant leader:

1. Listening
2. Empathy
3. Healing
4. Awareness
5. Persuasion
6. Conceptualization
7. Foresight
8. Stewardship
9. Commitment to the growth of people
10. Building community

## TRAINING AND EDUCATION

Leadership development requires training and education. Successful community leaders and organizers will make the development and offering of leadership training programs a part of their leadership agenda.

### Teaching

Successful community leaders and organizers should teach in leadership programs. Teaching sets a good example and is also an informal venue for modeling leadership. It helps the teacher become an even better leader, as she or he distills the leadership experience and extracts lessons learned to share with students.

Of course, the successful leader should not be the only instructor; community leadership should be broadly representative in such programs. One important point to remember is that teachers do not have to know everything; they just have to know one thing. This is the one-room-schoolhouse model. If you know fractions, you can teach younger children fractions, even if fractions are all you know.

### Project Learning

Projects are a good way to teach leadership because they are focused, are time bound, and have observable results. They offer newer leaders-in-development an opportunity to exercise nascent skills without taking on too much responsibility too soon. The relatively short-term nature of these assignments, together with their defined, observable results, means that older leaders can quickly offer reinforcement and, if the young leader encounters problems, relatively low negative effects. Projects can be focused on community betterment or personal betterment. Although these goals may seem quite disparate, some projects may actually contribute to both goals.

## Mentorship

Emerging leaders need mentorship, so successful community organizers and leaders can count on always mentoring at least one or two. Mentorship provides informal guidance to young leaders and assists them in selecting what projects to undertake and in what order. Mentoring also allows young leaders time for and feedback on personal after-action reviews and lessons-learned activities.

## LEADERS ARE EVERYWHERE

As one thinks about emerging leaders, questions of "Who are they?" and "Where are they?" often arise. The answer is, everyone and everywhere. Successful community leaders and organizers are always recruiting, with an open mind. Because they have broad contacts, they also have the opportunity to observe a wide range of community participants. Part of their gift is noticing who shows up, who gets things done, who can bring people together on common ground, who is tough when necessary, and who is supportive when support is needed. Emerging leaders are always present if we keep our eyes open. They may be young; they may be moms at home; they may be retired older adults; they may be busy professionals, craftspeople, or seasonal visitors. They may be, and are, everywoman and everyman. Emerging leaders are often waiting to be asked to do more. Because they are "emerging" they may hesitate to promote themselves into the community leadership and organizing system for fear of offending current leadership or appearing too pushy. That emerging leaders tend to hang back is yet another reason for developing an emerging leadership cadre.

## LEGACY

Successful community leaders and organizers have gained much experience and insight during their leadership. Unfortunately, in a large majority of instances, loosely coupled community systems lack a mechanism to capture this knowledge and experience and transfer it to emerging leaders. So communities and citizens spend much effort reinventing a wheel, rather than improving the wheel it already built.

Successful community leaders and organizers should always be interested in passing the torch, especially if they have had long careers. In fact, sharing expertise is essential. To accomplish this, leaders need to be comfortable with intergenerational leadership sharing. But it requires self-permission, something that some leaders feel good about but many do not, thinking that it violates Collins's (2005) humility rule and does not seem to fit the servant–leadership concept. In this case, a little ego (knowing that you have something to share) is a good thing; too much ego (thinking you have nothing to learn) causes trouble.

## CONCLUSION

The patterns and structures needed to prepare emerging leaders will vary from community to community. A few suggested foci are mentioned here, but others will develop depending on the community in question. Whatever the demographic mix, leaders are there. Our communities and our country are desperate at this time for broad-based leadership that can work locally and nationally to help us to adapt something like the U.S. Army recruiting slogan "Be All You Can Be"—and more.

# Appendix A
## Sample Agenda

To:     Community Group
From:   Pam
Re:     Community Meeting, Monday, 10 a.m.–12 p.m.
Date:   "Any Monday"

| | |
|---|---|
| 1. Announcements | 10:00–10:10 |
| *Penny, Sarah, Jessica, Matt* | |
| | |
| 2. Minutes from last meeting | 10:10–10:15 |
| | |
| 3. Easy Items (Decision) | 10:15–10:35 |
| 3a. Main Street decoration, *Penny* | 10:15–10:25 |

3. Easy Items (Decision) — 10:15–10:35
   3a. Main Street decoration, *Penny* — 10:15–10:25
   - The same firm is recommended to do the work as last year.
   3b. New music programs, *Matt* — 10:25–10:35
   - Matt recommends we invite the Marine Band from Washington, DC, for summer festival.

4. Moderately Tough Items (Decision)
   4a. Breast cancer alert, *Sarah* — 10:35–10:50
   - Mammography sites will be set up around town.

   4b.  Community archives, *Jessica*                  10:50–11:05
          • Review and approval is needed of new
             information system. (See Attachment A)

5. Tough Item (Decision)                                11:05–11:30
       • Approve negotiations for child welfare agency merger.

6. Blue-Sky Items (Discussion Only)                     11:30–12:00
       • Look at new issues.
       • Community Health Needs Software, *Matt*
       • Health online, *Jessica*
       • The health care system, *Sarah*

**Snack follows at noon!**

# Appendix B
## Sample Options Memo

THE PROBLEM

Community archives: Multiple storage locations for important documents.

KEY NEEDS

- Assessment reports for the community are stored in several agencies.
- A master file system has not yet been set up.
- There is lack of understanding about what should be stored and conflict over common locations.
- Thus, access is inhibited.

THE OPTIONS

1. Let things stay as they are for now.
2. Plan to revisit this problem in six months.
3. Ask Jessica to develop a plan for selection, storage, and access.

THE RECOMMENDATION: OPTION 3

- Jessica should be asked to develop a plan for selecting key documents and proposing a common storage location.
- In addition, she should propose ideas to improve access.
- Any delay means more will be lost and the job will be tougher.

# Appendix C
## Sample Minutes

1. Announcements
   Penny announced the new slot in the parking lot was now available for community meeting members. Sarah announced a new program at Woman's Health, Inc. Matt announced he would be at a software meeting on Friday. Jessica announced new materials for the library.

2. Minutes from Last Monday's Meeting
   The minutes for the last meeting were accepted.

3. Decision Items

3a. Community Decoration
   The firm used last year was thought to be satisfactory; there is no price increase for this year.

3b. New Music Program
   Matt knows several people in the President's own Marine Band in Washington, DC. He feels it is possible to get on their tour schedule. It was agreed to proceed.

4a. Mobile Mammography
   Problems have occurred in the community because women live too far from mammography services. Sarah will look into transportation

services and has arranged for portable mammography units to be available on a preannounced schedule.

4b. Community Archives
There was discussion of the community archives report. We will proceed with the development of a new information system.

5. Child Welfare Agency Merger Negotiations
Given the economic climate, it seemed useful for our community group to urge the two child welfare agencies in town to explore merger possibilities. Both are opposed; neither is interested in even talking to the other. This resistance was taken as an excellent reason to proceed. Other reasons include community complaints about each, the shabby quarters each has, and the real possibility of running one excellent organization.

6. Blue Sky Items: New Markets
A lively discussion of new issues (software, health online, and health care settings) was held. Each of these seemed promising. More discussion will be held next month.

# Appendix D
## Resources for Research

A dapted from "Researching Advocacy Groups: Internet Sources for Research about Public Interest Groups and Social Movement Organizations" (McNutt, 2010).

### GENERAL RESOURCES

Several sources provide overviews of advocacy organizations. The Urban Institute, which has had a long-term interest in advocacy, hosts a Web site with a variety of resources about advocacy efforts, particularly those involving children (http://www2.urban.org/advocacyresearch/).

The American Political Science Association maintains a Political Organizations and Parties Section Homepage (httpi/www.apsanet. org/—pop), which contains a great deal of helpful information. The American Sociological Association's Section on Social Movements (http://www2.asanet. org/sectioncbsm/) is another useful resource. So, too, is the Web site devoted to Women and Social Movements in the United States, which provides excellent historical material (http://womhist.alexanderstreet.com/).

Individual scholars also maintain Web sites that provide information on advocacy organizations. Professor Marshall Ganz's Practicing Democracy Network contains material including syllabi, directories, course notes, and papers (http://www.hks.harvard.edu/organizing/). The Protest Page of Professor Susan Oliver contains many of her own resources, as

well as links to additional material on other sites (http://www.ssc.wisc.
edu/). Links from Professor Frank Baumgartner's faculty Web site are
also an excellent source of information (http://www.unc.edu/–Ibaum/).

Resources related to international advocacy can be found at the
United Nations Research Institute for Social Development, Civil Society, and Social Movements Program (http://www.unrisd.org); the World
Bank (http://www.worldbank.org); and the Brookings Institution (http://
www.brookings.edu/).

### Identifying Advocacy Organizations and Organizational Financing

The Internet provides a range of resources for identifying advocacy
organizations. For domestic groups, the Urban Institute's National Center for Charitable Statistics is a good source of information (http://nccs.
urban.org/). So, too, is Guidestar (http://www2.guidestar.org), which also
includes IRS Form 990s in its database for those organizations that are
both corporations and have an IRS Tax Status. These Web sites provide
information about the sources of funding for the organization in question. Similar information is also available from the Center for Responsive
Politics' Open Secrets Web site (http://www.opensecrets.org). When organizations engage in the electoral process, they must file with the Federal
Election Commission (http://www.fec.gov).

However, unincorporated associations rarely show up in such listings,
and they must be found by searching for the organizational Web sites.

Transnational organizations are also difficult to find, but a good
source (or a good place to start) is World Advocacy (http://www.world
advocacy.com).

### Advocacy Activity and Lobbyists

Two organizations, the Alliance for Justice (http://www.afj.org/) and
Charity Lobbying in the Public Interest (http://www.clpi.org/), provide
detailed information on what types of activity are prohibited and permit-
ted by law.

The Honest Leadership and Open Government Act of 2007 (P.L. 110-
81) and the Lobbying Disclosure Act (P.L. 104-339) set the parameters
for lobbying registration, prohibited activities, and reporting, and they
require that reporting data be electronically available. These reports

are available from the U.S. Senate (http://www.senate.gov/legislative/
resources/pdf/S1guidance.pdf) and the U.S. House of Representatives
(http://lobbyingdisclosure.house.gov/). Information on lobbying activity
is also provided by Open Secrets (www.opensecrets.org/lobbyisrs/) and
the Center for Public Integrity (http://projects.publicintegrity.org/lobby/).

Information on lobbying by foreign organizations in American politics
can be found through the Foreign Lobbying Influence Tracker (http://
foreignlobbying.org/), a project of ProPublica and the Sunlight Founda-
tion, which organizes information about these efforts. The U.S. Department of Justice's Foreign Agent Registration Act (22 U.S.C. § 611 et seq.)
information page (http://www.fara.gov/) includes a database, and copies
of the annual reports that it provides to Congress.

Most states provide access to lobbying registration information. This
information is generally available either on the state legislature's Web site
or on the Web site of the state agency that regulates lobbying.

### Other Resources for Discovering Advocacy Activities

Protest Net (http://www.protest.net) is a running guide to demonstrations and other actions, organized by issues and locations.

Sourcewatch (http://www.sourcewatch.org) is a project of the Center
for Media and Democracy that provides information on organizations
attempting to influence public policy through the media.

OMBWatch (www.ombwatch.org) has created FedSpending.org (www.
fedspending.org/) to share information about federal spending and provide a picture of who benefits from federal legislation.

Topix (http://www.topix.com/news/activism) follows news stories related
to activism and advocacy.

## ADDITIONAL RESOURCES

Andrews, K., & Edwards, B. (2004). Advocacy organizations in the U.S. policy
process. *Annual Review of Sociology, 30,* 479–506.
Barcus, J., & Wilkinson, J. (1995). *Handbook of management consulting services.* New York: McGraw-Hill.

Bernard, J. (1968). Community disorganization. In D. Sills (Ed.), *International encyclopedia of the social sciences* (Vol. 3, pp. 163–169). New York: Free Press.

Berry, J. M., & Arons, D. F. (2002). *A voice for nonprofits.* Washington, DC: Brookings Institution Press.

Boris, E. T., & Mosher-Williams, R. (1998). Nonprofit advocacy organizations: Assessing the definitions, classifications, and data. *Nonprofit and Voluntary Sector Quarterly, 27,* 488–506.

Burghart, S. (1965). Know yourself: A key to better organizing. In J. Tropman, J. Erlich, & J. Rothman (Eds.), *Tactics and techniques of community intervention* (3rd ed., pp. 56–62). Itasca, IL: F. E. Peacock.

Burghardt, S. (1987). Community-based social action. In A. Minahan (Ed-in-Chief), *Encyclopedia of social work* (18th ed., Vol. 1, pp. 292–299). Silver Spring, MD: National Association of Social Workers.

Burk, E. (1965). The search for authority in planning. *Social Service Review, 39,* 261–270.

Child, C. P., & Gronbjerg, I.C.A. (2007). Nonprofit advocacy organizations: Their characteristics and activities. *Social Science Quarterly, 88*(1), 259–281.

Davis, S., & Botkin, J. (1994). *The monster under the bed.* New York: Simon & Schuster.

Ezeil, M. (2001). *Advocacy in the human services.* Belmont, CA: Wadsworth.

Fellin, P. (2000). *The community and the social worker* (3rd ed.). Itasca, IL: F. E. Peacock.

Gavin, P., & Gelak, O. (2008). Lobbying disclosure databases. *Online, 32*(5), 34–38.

Greenleaf Center for Servant Leadership. (2011). *What is servant leadership?* Retrieved from http://www.greenleaf.org/whatissl/

Haynes, K., & Mickelson, J. (2003). *Affecting change: Social workers in the political arena* (5th ed.). Boston: Allyn & Bacon.

Hoefet, R. (2000). Making a difference: Human service interest group influence on social welfare program regulations. *Journal of Sociology and Social Welfare, 27*(3), 21–38.

King, R. (1997). *Deep change.* San Francisco: Jossey-Bass.

Lane, R. (1940). Report of groups studying the community organization process. In E. Day (Ed.), *Proceedings of the National Conference of Social Work, 1940* (p. 456). New York: Columbia University Press.

Lippit, R., Watson, H. J., & Westley, B. (1958). *The dynamics of planned change.* New York: Harcourt, Brace and World.

Lipset, S. M. (1979). *The first new nation.* New York: W. W. Norton.

Reeser, L. C. (1992). Professional role orientation and social activism. *Journal of Sociology and Social Welfare, 19*(2), 79–94.

Ross, M. G. (1955). *Community organization.* New York: Harper Bros.

Ross, M. G. (1958). *Case histories in community organization.* New York: Harper Bros.

Rothman, J. (1995). Approaches to community intervention. In J. Rothman, J. Erlich, & J. Tropman (Eds.), *Strategies of community organization* (5th ed., pp. 26–63). Itasca, IL: F. E. Peacock.

Rothman, J., Tropman, J., & Erlich, J. (2007). *Strategies of community practice* (7th ed.). Peosta, IA: Eddie Bowers.

Schneider, R. L., & Lester, L. (2001). *Social work advocacy: A new framework for action.* Belmont, CA: Brooks/Cole.

Schwartz, M. (1965). Community organization. In H. L. Lurie (Ed.), *Encyclopedia of social work* (15th ed., pp. 177–190). New York: National Association of Social Workers.

Spergel, I. A. (1987). Community development. In A. Minahan (Ed.-in-Chief), *Encyclopedia of social work* (18th ed., Vol. 1, pp. 299–308). Silver Spring, MD: National Association of Social Workers.

Weil, M. (Ed.). (1996). *Community practice: Conceptual models.* Binghamton, NY: Haworth Press.

Weil, M. (Ed.). (in press). *Community practice: Models in action.* Binghamton, NY: Haworth Press.

West, O. M. (2006). *Digital government: Technology and public sector performance.* Princeton, NJ: Princeton University Press.

See also many articles on community in R. L. Edwards (Ed.-in-Chief), (1995), *Encyclopedia of social work* (20th ed.). Washington, DC: NASW Press.

## Web Site

http://www.logcabin.org/site/c.nsKSL7PMLpF/b.5468093/k.BE4C/Home.htm


## REFERENCES

Alinsky, S. (1946). *Reveille for radicals.* Chicago: University of Chicago Press.

Alinsky, S. (1971). *Rules for radicals.* New York: Random House.

Alinsky, S. (1992). *Let them call me rebel.* New York: Vintage.

Argyris, C. (1985). Strategy, change, and defensive routines. Boston: Pitman.

Bailey, R. (1976). *The Alinsky approach.* Chicago: University of Chicago Press.

Baker, W. (1994). *Networking smart: How to build relationships for business and personal success.* New York: McGraw Hill.

Bell, J. (1995). *The activist and the alienated.* In P. Schervish, V. A. Hodgkinson, M. Gates & Associates (Eds.), *Care and community in modern society: Passing on the tradition of service to future generations* (pp. 144–153). San Francisco: Jossey-Bass.

Bernard, J. (1968). Community disorganization. In D. Sills (Ed.), *International encyclopedia of the social sciences* (Vol. 3, pp. 163–169). New York: Free Press.

Black, C. (1981). *It will never happen to me.* New York: Ballantine Books.

Bolton, R. (1986). *People skills: How to assert yourself, listen to others, and resolve conflicts.* New York: Simon & Schuster.

Boorstin, D. (1958). *The Americans: The colonial experience.* New York: Random House.

Bramson, R. M. (1981). *Coping with difficult people.* New York: Ballantine Books.

Burghardt, S. (2001). Know yourself: A key to better organizing. In J. E. Tropman, J. L. Erlich, & J. Rothman (Eds.), *Tactics and techniques of community intervention* (4th ed., pp. 150–156). Itasca, IL: F. E. Peacock.

Burk, E. (1965). The search for authority in planning. *Social Service Review, 39,* 261–270.

Chua, A. (2011). *Battle hymn of the tiger mother.* New York: Penguin Press.

Cohen, M., March, J., & Olson, J. (1972). A garbage can model of organizational choice. *Administrative Science Quarterly, 17,* 1–25.

Collins, J. (2005). Level 5 leadership: The triumph of humility and fierce resolve. *Harvard Business Review, 83* (7–8), 136–146. Retrieved from http://hbr.org/2005/07/level-5-leadership/ar/1

Community informatics. (2011). *Wikipedia, the free encyclopedia.* Retrieved from http://en.wikipedia.org/wiki/Community_informatics

Davis, S., & Botkin, J. (1994). *The monster under the bed.* New York: Simon & Schuster.

de Bono, E. (1985). *Six thinking hats.* New York: Little, Brown.

Deming, W. E. (1982). *Out of crisis.* Cambridge, MA: MIT Press.

de Tocqueville, A. C. (1841). *Democracy in America.* New York: Langley.

Deutch, M. (1968). Field theory. In D. Sills (Ed.), *International encyclopedia of the social sciences* (Vol. 5, pp. 406–417). New York: Free Press.

Dreyfus, H. L., & Dreyfus, S. E. (1986). *Mind over machine.* New York: Free Press.

Egan, G. (1994). *Working the shadow side.* San Francisco: Jossey-Bass.

Fellin, P. (2000). *The community and the social worker* (3rd ed.). Itasca, IL: F. E. Peacock.

Gamson, W. (1966). Rancorous conflict in community politics. *American Sociological Review, 31,* 71–81.

Garvin, C. D., & Cox, F. M. (1995). A history of community organization since the Civil War with special reference to oppressed communities. In J. Rothman, J. Erlich, & J. Tropman (Eds.), *Strategies of community intervention* (5th ed., pp. 64–98). Itasca, IL: F. E. Peacock.

Gladwell, M. (2008). *Outliers.* New York: Little, Brown.

Goleman, D. (2006). *Social intelligence: The new science of human relationships.* New York: Bantam Books.

Gummer, B. (1995). Social planning. In R. L. Edwards (Ed.-in-Chief), *Encyclopedia of social work* (19th ed., Vol. 3, pp. 2180–2186). Washington, DC: NASW Press.

Harvey, J. (1974). The Abilene paradox. *Organizational Dynamics,* pp. 63–80.

Hochschild, A. (2003). *The managed heart: The commercialization of human feeling.* Berkeley: University of California Press.

Hoffer, E. (1951). *The true believer.* New York: Harper.

Janis, I. (1983). *Groupthink: Psychological studies of policy decisions and fiascoes.* Boston: Houghton-Mifflin.

Jay, A. (2009). *How to run a meeting.* Cambridge, MA: Harvard Business School Press.

Johnson, H. R., & Tropman, J. E. (1979). The setting of community organization practice. In F. M. Cox, J. L. Erlich, J. Rothman, & J. E. Tropman (Eds.), *Strategies of community organization* (3rd ed., pp. 213–223). Itasca, IL: F. E. Peacock.

Jones, W. T. (1952). *History of Western philosophy.* New York: Harcourt Brace.

Kerr, S. (1975). On the folly of rewarding A while hoping for B. *Academy of Management Journal, 18,* 769–783.

Kiersey, D., & Bates, M. (1984). *Please understand me* (4th ed.). Del Mar, CA: Prometheus Nemesis.

King, R. (1997). *Deep change.* San Francisco: Jossey-Bass.

Lane, R. (1939). The field of community organization. In R. Kurtz (Ed.), *Proceedings of the National Conference of Social Work, 1939* (pp. 495–511). New York: Columbia University Press.

Leider, R., & Spears, L. (2009). *Savoring life through servant leadership.* Indianapolis: Larry G. Spears Center for Servant-Leadership. Retrieved from http://www.spearscenter.org/SAVORINGLIFE_fin.pdf

Log Cabin Republicans. (2011). "About us." http://www.logcabin.org/site/c.nsKSL7PMLpF/b.5468093/k.BE4C/Home.htm

Lowe, G. R. (1995). Social development. In R. L. Edwards (Ed.-in-Chief), *Encyclopedia of social work* (19th ed., Vol. 3, pp. 2168–2173). Washington, DC: NASW Press.

McNutt, J. G. (2010). Researching advocacy groups: Internet sources for research about public interest groups and social movement organizations. *Journal of Policy Practice, 9,* 308–312.

McNutt, J. G., & Boland, K. M. (2007). Astroturf, technology and the future of community mobilization: Implications for nonprofit theory. *Journal of Sociology and Social Welfare, 34*(3), 165–179.

Michels, R. (1949). *Political parties.* Glencoe, IL: Free Press.

Minnesota Department of Health (n.d.). *Types of evaluation.* Retrieved from http://www.health.state.mn.us/divs/hpcd/chp/hpkit/text/eval_types.htm

Myers, G. C. (1987). *When it hits the fan: Managing the nine crises of business.* New York: Signet.

Nepo, M. (2009). Welcoming reflections. In *Community resilience: A cross-cultural study* (pp. 7–9). Retrieved from http://www.fetzer.org/images/stories/pdf/wc1_final_cusp_commrespdf012812.pdf

Nierenberg, R. (2009). *Maestro: A surprising story about leading by listening.* New York: Penguin Group.

Prahalad, C. K. (2005). *The fortune at the bottom of the pyramid: Eradicating poverty through profits.* Upper Saddle River, NJ: Prentice Hall.

Putnam, R. (2000). *Bowling alone: The collapse and revival of American community.* New York: Simon & Schuster.

Quinn, R. E. (1988). *Beyond rational management: Mastering the paradoxes and competing demands of high performance.* San Francisco: Jossey-Bass.

Riesman, D. (1954). *Individualism reconsidered.* Glencoe, IL: Free Press.

Riesman, D., Glazer, N., & Denney, R. (1950). *The lonely crowd: A study of the changing character of America.* New Haven, CT: Yale University Press.

Robert, H. M. III (1970). *Robert's rules of order newly revised* (7th ed.). Glenview, IL: Scott, Foresman, Brown.

Rothman, J., Erlich, J., & Tropman, J. (Eds.). (1995). *Strategies of community organization* (5th ed.). Itasca, IL: F. E. Peacock.

Sayles, L. R., & Chandler, M. K. (1993). *Managing large systems: Organizations for the future.* New York: Harper & Row.

Schwartz, M. (1965). Community organization. In H. L. Lurie (Ed.), *Encyclopedia of social work* (15th ed., pp. 177–190). New York: National Association of Social Workers.

Sen, A. (1992). *Inequality reexamined.* Cambridge, MA: Harvard University Press.

Simon, H., Thompson, V., & Smithburg, D. (1991). *Public administration.* New Brunswick, NJ: Transaction Publications.

Spergel, I. (1987). Community development. In A. Minahan (Ed.-in-Chief), *Encyclopedia of social work* (18th ed., Vol. 1, pp. 299–308). Silver Spring, MD: National Association of Social Workers.

Tichy, N. M., & Devanna, M. A. (1986). *The transformational leader.* San Francisco: John Wiley & Sons.

Tropman, J. E. (1971). Staffing committees and studies. In F. M. Cox, J. Erlich, J. Rothman, & J. Tropman (Eds.), *Tactics and techniques of community practice* (pp. 105–111). Itasca, IL: F. E. Peacock.

Tropman, J. E. (1984). *Policy management in the human services.* New York: Columbia University Press.

Tropman, J. E. (1995). Community needs assessment. In R. L. Edwards (Ed.), *Encyclopedia of social work* (19th ed., Vol. 1, pp. 563–569). Washington, DC: NASW Press.

Tropman, J. E. (2006). *Meetings: How to make them work for you.* Thousand Oaks, CA. Sage Publications.

Tropman, J. E., & Wooten L. (2010). Executive leadership: A 7C approach. *Problems and Perspectives in Management, 8*(4), 47–57.

Tuchman, B. (1984). *The march of folly.* New York: Knopf.

Video Arts. (Producer). (1976). *Meetings, bloody meetings* [Video]. Retrieved from http://www.media-partners.com/business_meetings/meetings_bloody_ meetings_training_video.htm

Vinter, R., & Tropman, J. (1971). The causes and consequences of community studies. In F. M. Cox, J. Erlich, J. Rothman, & J. Tropman (Eds.), *Tactics and techniques of community organization* (pp. 315–322). Itasca, IL: F E. Peacock.

Weil, M. O., & Gamble, D. N. (1995). Community practice models. In R. L. Edwards (Ed.-in-Chief), *Encyclopedia of social work* (19th ed., Vol. 1, pp. 577–594). Washington, DC: NASW Press.

Wilensky, H., & Lebeaux, C. (1956). *Industrial society and social welfare.* New York: Russell Sage.

# Index

In this index, *f* denotes figure and *t* denotes table.

# About the Author

JOHN E. TROPMAN, PHD, MSW, is professor, School of Social Work, University of Michigan, Ann Arbor, where he teaches in the areas of human services management, community organization, and social policy and in the joint doctoral program in social work and social science. He has written and edited a number of books in the areas of management, community organization, and social policy: Creating and sustaining caring, constructive communities through the appropriate leadership has been one of his lifetime interests.